# THE IDEAL OF THE MONASTIC LIFE
# FOUND IN THE APOSTOLIC AGE

# The Ideal
OF THE
# Monastic Life
# Found in the Apostolic Age

❧

# Dom Germain Morin, O.S.B
OF THE ABBEY OF MAREDSOUS

TRANSLATED FROM THE FRENCH BY
## C. GUNNING

WITH A PREFACE BY
## DOM BEDE CAMM, O.S.B.
OF DOWNSIDE ABBEY

**CANA PRESS**

I hereby approve of Dom Germain Morin's book, "L'Idéal Monastique et la Vie Chrétienne des Premiers Jours," and authorise its translation into English according to arrangements made with Dom Bede Camm, O.S.B.
✠ COLUMBA MARMION,
Abbot of Maredsous,
Die 30 Octobris, 1913

*Nihil Obstat*
FR. INNOCENTIUS APAP., O.P.
CENSOR DEPUTATUS

*Imprimatur*
EDM. CAN. SURMONT,
VICARIUS GENERALIS
13th November, 1913

First Published by
Benziger Brothers
New York, Cincinnati, Chicago

Newly revised and edited
Special thanks to T.P. Garvey
Cana Press © 2021
All rights reserved

For information, address:
PO Box 85
Colebrook,
Tasmania, 7027,
Australia
notredamemonastery.org

ISBN
978-0-6488688-7-3

# CONTENTS

| | |
|---|---|
| Original Editor's Preface | vii |
| Preface | ix |
| Vocation: Compunction of Heart | 1 |
| Obedience | 11 |
| Penance | 25 |
| Baptism and Profession | 37 |
| The Apostolic Life | 49 |
| The Breaking of Bread | 61 |
| Liturgical Prayer | 73 |
| Monastic Spirituality | 85 |
| Monastic Poverty | 97 |
| Discretion and Breadth of View | 107 |
| Joy | 117 |
| Simplicity | 129 |

# ORIGINAL EDITOR'S PREFACE

I HAVE BEEN ASKED by the Abbot of Maredsous to prepare this translation of Dom Germain Morin's work for the press, and to write a few words of introduction. I cannot refuse one to whom I owe so much, but it is obviously quite unnecessary, if not impertinent, for me to say anything in commendation of either the author or his book.

Dom Morin has a European reputation as a savant, and the University of Oxford has honoured not so much him as itself in giving him a Doctor's degree *honoris causa.* His discoveries in the field of patristic study, his illuminating treatment, to take only one example, of the problem of the authorship of the *Quicunque vult,* his enormous labours in preparing a complete and final edition of the works of St. Caesarius of Arles, his brilliant studies on the most difficult questions of liturgical research, have indeed made his name famous in the annals of erudition. The French edition of this work was published anonymously, but the present writer has been fortunate enough to succeed in persuading the learned author to allow his name to appear in this translation.

To those who do not know Dom Morin, save as a savant, these simple pages may come as a revelation.

For here we find no parade of erudition, no affectation of research. We have the humble and devout monk speaking simply and earnestly, to his brethren in the cloister, of the eternal truths and of those special obligations which the monastic life imposes. The whole work breathes the simple piety of the ages of faith, and is impregnated with that peace of heart and liberty of spirit which are characteristic of the true son of St. Benedict.

Yes, this is no mere collection of pious exhortations; it is a work full of solid doctrine founded on the Benedictine Rule, and on the writings of the Saints and Fathers, by one who has drunk deeply of their spirit.

If we read these pages attentively, we shall be more and more impressed by the fact that, simple as they seem, they are very far from being commonplace, but are indeed the fruit of no ordinary mind. Only one, in fact, who, like Dom Morin, was deeply versed in the annals of monastic antiquity could possibly have written them.

The present writer had the happiness of being a member of the Community to whom these meditations were first addressed. It was his very first retreat as a Catholic, and he has never forgotten it. Some of the meditations, especially, perhaps, that on the analogy between Baptism and the Monastic Ceremony of Profession, left an impression on his mind which has never been effaced. It is therefore to him a special pleasure to introduce this work to the English-speaking world.

It will be found most useful, not merely to Benedictines, for whom it was first intended, not merely to religious, for whom it has so many precious lessons, but to all Christians who are interested in those eternal verities which were at once the strength and consolation of our fathers in the faith, and in those great and sacred principles which formed in the Benedictine cloister such giants of sanctity as Gregory, Anselm, and Dunstan, to whom Christendom in general and England in particular owe so enormous a debt.

DOM BEDE CAMM,
*Monk of Downside Abbey.*
*Feast of St. Dunstan, April* 19, 1914.

# PREFACE

About twenty years ago a certain Benedictine Abbot suddenly ordered one of his monks, still young and inexperienced, to deliver before an important community the conferences usual in the course of the annual Retreat.

As this Retreat coincided with the week of Pentecost, the monk thought that he could not do better than demonstrate, from the manner of life of the primitive Christians immediately after the descent of the Spirit, the origin and model of the life that should be led by monks. So he took for his text the verses from the Acts of the Apostles 2:37-46, not commenting upon the whole passage in order, but confining himself to the principal features which referred to his subject.

The notes which he made for these conferences were for a long time forgotten, unless occasionally one of his brethren used them for giving spiritual exercises in his turn.

Certainly, if the author had followed his own feeling, they would never have been used at all. But lately he has been obliged to consent that the substance of them should be published in a little review, called the *Messenger of Saint Benedict*, and this first publication, although fragmentary and mixed up here and there with sketches on different subjects, has aroused in a certain number of people a strong desire to see the whole collected and brought out in its original form.

After having resisted as long as he possibly could, the author at last gave way, thinking that it was his duty to put aside his personal disinclination for the sake of the spiritual advantage of his neighbour, which, he was told, rightly or wrongly, was concerned in this publication.

Naturally, certain details have been eliminated which belonged to the particular conditions of the audience for whom these pages were prepared. But, on the other hand, the references of most of the texts and quotations have been added in notes. Of most of them only; for there are some which come from purely oral instruction—from Dom Gueranger, for example; from Maurus Wolter, and other great monks of our time. The author has no longer within his reach the works from which he borrowed two or three other quotations without always noting accurately the place whence they were taken. The reader must be so good as to trust him on this point, and believe that everything that he attributes to an author is really by that author. Having made the search for and worship of the truth the principal business of his life, he would never allow himself to deceive in this matter, even with a view to edification.

Neither must it be forgotten that these pages were written long ago, and many points would have required completion. Perhaps, on the other hand, certain pages would not appear, if they had been written more recently. After all, there will not be much cause to complain of that. Origen says, in his eighteenth Homily on Exodus, that the preacher of the Gospel should have that enthusiasm and youthfulness of soul attributed to Judah in the "Blessings of the Patriarchs"—*may his eyes be red from wine.*\*

No coldness, no feebleness, no colourlessness in his language; but a kind of holy inebriation, something that rejoices the friends of God and heals the wounds of the soul.

\* *Oculi ejus rubri a vino.*

Happy are they who have received this gift of spiritual youth, and the power of communicating it! Happy, above all, are they, and much more rare, who have known how to preserve and cherish it, even to old age.

*Ash Wednesday,* 1912.

# I
# VOCATION: COMPUNCTION OF HEART

*His autem auditis compuncti sunt corde*
"When they had heard these things they had
compunction in their heart" (Acts 2:37).

IT IS THE DAY of Pentecost. The Holy Ghost has come down upon the Apostles; the Church has been founded. But this Church, which is to fill the whole world, is as yet so small that the Cenacle suffices to contain it. How will the Holy Spirit act in order to make of this insignificant stone that great mountain foretold by the prophet Daniel? (*cf.* Dan 2:35).

What elements will He bring into play powerful enough to unite to this handful of men all the predestinate in the confused mass of the human race? Let us contemplate Him at His work. It is He who speaks by the mouth of Peter: "O ye Jews," he says, "my brethren of the house of Israel, hearken! This Jesus of Nazareth whom you have taken, and given up into the hands of wicked men, whom God hath raised up, is the Lord, the Messiah: and you, again I say, have crucified Him" *(cf.* Acts 2:14-36). Here, certainly, is an arrow which seems made to wound, to pierce to the quick: and truly it strikes home. But see how salutary is this wound! Far from being irritated, from protesting, from silencing Peter, these men who, a few weeks before, had been steeped in the awful crime of Deicide, now strike their breasts: they are touched with compunction. *They had compunction in their heart.*\* Compunction, therefore, is the first fruit which the Holy Ghost produces in the souls of those whom He calls to the Christian Faith.

\* *Compuncti sunt corde.*

It is also the first and surest sign of a monastic vocation. The monk is a Christian who renounces the ordinary life of men, that he may embrace one more perfect. Now, under what influences does he resolve to make this change? This is well expressed in one of the prayers prescribed in our Ritual for the clothing of novices: O God, grant the gift of perseverance to Thy servant, whom Thou hast separated from other men by enkindling in his heart the fire of holy compunction—*Quem sanctae compunctionis ardore ab hominum ceterorum proposito segregasti.*

It is, then, the spirit of compunction which must direct the first steps of the soul who turns from the broad way of the world to follow the narrow path of perfection. This was clearly the idea of St Benedict; and, lest we should forget it, lest we should dare to cross the threshold of the monastery without this indispensable companion, he begins his Rule—the first book which will be put into our hands—by reproaching us for our past cowardice: *from whom thou hast strayed by the sloth of disobedience.*\* He consents to receive us on this sole condition: that we should acknowledge and deplore our cowardice, and be ready to make amends for it. And to help us the better to enter into these sentiments, he solemnly orders, in another place, that the novice who desires conversion should be met with rebuffs, believing this to be the best method of "trying the spirits." He knows that no one can endure these difficulties if he have not the spirit of compunction, and that, on the other hand, to begin without this spirit would be to expose himself, sooner or later, to a fall.

But even when we have entered the monastery in and through this spirit, we cannot, without it, either persevere or make any true progress. For it is a law, established by God Himself, that every creature must seek his natural means of subsistence from the source whence he first received his being.

\* *A quo per inoboedientiae desidiam recesseras.*

This is why the holy Rule recommends the use of that salutary question, *Why have you come?*\* Why have we come to the monastic life? What has impelled us to it? The spirit of compunction. The best means, then, of securing our perseverance is constantly to renew this spirit within us, and this is one of the principal objects of our yearly spiritual exercises.

The word compunction comes from the Latin verb *pungere*, which means "to prick." Compunction is a pricking of the soul; this implies that it is a suffering, for there are few pains to which we are more sensitive than to a prick. But this suffering has this peculiarity, that usually it is voluntary: only those feel it who willingly inflict it on themselves, or at least lay their souls open to its stings.

The state of compunction is, to the soul, what those cuirasses lined with sharp points, of which we read in the lives of great penitents, are to the body. The soul which has reached this state can no longer make the slightest movement without reopening her wound. Other souls, weaker or less advanced, feel these more painful stings but rarely, and not on all sides; compunction in them is like those crosses furnished with points, those bracelets and cinctures which some Christians wear in penitential seasons. The pain is less severe; but in the main it is the same thing—a pricking of the soul.

Now, what is the weapon whose point is keen enough to penetrate the innermost depths of the soul? St Paul tells us there is "a sword of the Spirit which is the word of God" (Eph. 6:17). "For the word of God," as the same Apostle says in another place, "is living and effectual, and more piercing than any two-edged sword: reaching unto the division of the soul and spirit, of the joints also and marrow" (Heb. 4:12). Was it not this sword of the word of God which touched the three thou-

\* *Ad quid venisti?*

sand hearers who were converted by the voice of Peter? Did not the Apostle draw the sword of Holy Writ against them when he showed them how the oracles of David and the Prophets had been fulfilled in Christ, and how they themselves, by that very fact, were become Deicides, destined, if they would not repent, to be made a footstool for their Victim, exalted at the right hand of the Father? Such was the discourse which, to use St Luke's forcible words, cut them to the heart.

There are many ways in which the Divine word may triumph over the hardness of our hearts, and make in them an entrance for holy compunction. By some, this word may be found in the armoury of the Scriptures; by others, heard in the voice of Superiors or those commissioned to teach; or, finally, it may come directly from the Spirit of God, Who, filling the universe, and containing all things in His immensity, well knows how to make His Voice heard at that very moment which His mercy has willed.

In all these cases, since the first impulse must come from God, working in the soul of each one of us, our clear duty is to remove whatever may obstruct or extinguish the operations of the Holy Spirit: such as dissipation, idle talking, too frequent or excessive laughter, useless relations with the outside world; above all, ingratitude—ingratitude towards God—these are so many causes of trouble which dry up the springs of compunction, and against which St Benedict, in his Rule, repeatedly puts us on our guard.

Who can read, without seeing into the very depths of his great soul, that sixth chapter in which the spirit of silence—*taciturnitatis gravitas*—is inculcated on us in terms which have left their impress on all Christian ages; where an excommunication, absolute and perpetual—*aeterna clausura*—is pronounced against buffoonery and idle words, good only to promote laughter?

Of course, we know the true spirit of the holy Patriarch too well to conclude from these passages that he wished utterly to banish from our monasteries those outward manifestations of joy which are part of man's very nature, and which, if rightly used, may (through charity above all) so easily be raised to the rank of supernatural virtues. But we must always bear *this* in mind, that the strong terms here employed by our Lawgiver would at once find their justification, if ever (which God forbid) the spirit of compunction should suffer by these necessary alleviations accorded to nature.

This consideration is particularly important for those who have just come to the monastery, or who have not been long there; for it is certain that the soil of their souls will never be sufficiently tilled, and that the transformation which must needs be wrought in them will be seriously hindered, if they do not apply themselves (especially in these early days) to recollection, modesty, and silence. It behoves them, above all, strenuously to use those three precious instruments of spiritual art: *Not to love much speaking. Not to speak with vain words or such as move to laughter. Not to love much or violent laughter*\* (Rule, ch. 4). They cannot, of course, with all their efforts, arrive at once at the perfect practice of the ninth, tenth, and eleventh degrees of humility corresponding to these instruments; but they can, and they must, attain at least to that exterior result without which it is impossible to plant their feet firmly, even upon the first step, which is the fear of God.

But again, this being only the negative side, is insufficient: we must labour diligently to establish in ourselves the holy spirit of compunction, and to do this we need not seek farther than the admirable monastic code.

\* *Multum loqui non amare. Verba vana aut risui apta non loqui. Risum multum aut excussum non amare.*

The great means is Prayer. It is when treating of prayer that the blessed Father speaks of compunction and tears. Nothing, in fact, conduces more to win for us these inestimable gifts than prayer, whether the name be taken in its strict sense, or whether we understand by it the habitual thought of the presence of God, and the various spiritual exercises which succeed one another throughout the day.

What, indeed, is prayer but the soul ascending towards God, and thereby exposing herself to the shafts of Him, Who, as the Psalmist says, holds "those sharp arrows which are able to subdue whole nations under His feet?" (Ps 44:6).

Now, the arrows of the Divine Spouse are of four kinds *(cf* Gregory, *Morals,* I., 23., n. 41), all forged out of fear and love; in suchwise, however, that in the first two fear chiefly enters, whilst the last two are almost entirely love.

The first kind of shaft is intended to make the soul realize her past state, *ubi fuit*—that is to say, her former sins, her abuse of God's benefits, and her numberless infidelities. From this follows that compunction which overflowed the heart of the Publican, when, not daring even to lift up his eyes, he humbly repeated that cry which was sufficient to justify him: *O God, be merciful to me a sinner.*\* St Benedict suggests this practice to us, when he tells us never to let a day pass without, in our prayers, confessing our past sins to God, with tears and sighs: *Daily in one's prayer, with tears and sighs, to confess one's past sins to God*† (Rule, ch. 4.). The same wish is expressed in the Preface which the Abbot sings over the newly professed: *May he unceasingly with tears accuse his sins.*‡

---

\* *Deus propitius esto mihi peccatori.*
† *Mala sua praeterita cum lacrimis vel gemitu cotidie in oratione Deo confiteri.*
‡ *Peccata sua incessabiliter cum lacrimis accusit.*

We may all feel this first kind of compunction, for, as St John tells us, "if any man say that he is without sin, he deceiveth himself, and the truth is not in him" (1 John 1:8). We know, moreover, that it is not necessary to have committed great crimes in order to feel a high degree of compunction at the remembrance of past faults; we need only call to mind those touching prayers of our own St Anselm, in which this grief breaks out into veritable sobs, although there is nothing in his life to indicate such errors as we might be led to imagine.

The tears of true compunction are like a magnifying-glass, continually discovering to the inward eye new faults hitherto unperceived, and revealing to it more and more of their malice.

The second kind of compunction springs from fear of the punishment merited by sin; the guilty soul considers the sentence to be pronounced at the last day, and trembles as she asks herself where will *her* place be, *ubi erit*. St Paul himself, that great Apostle who was raised to the third heaven, knew this salutary terror, and feared lest he should be among the reprobate: *ne forte aliis praedicans ipse reprobus efficiar* (1 Cor. 9:27).

We must admit that after such an example it would ill become us to dispense ourselves from this fear, all the more because Scripture teaches us that "no one can be certain whether he be worthy of love or hatred" (Eccles, 9:1). I do not know, but to me it seems most difficult for a truly Christian soul to hear without trembling those threats which the holy Gospels sound so often in our ears: "Cast him into the exterior darkness; there shall be weeping and gnashing of teeth" (Matt. 22:13, etc.). "Depart from Me, ye cursed, into everlasting fire" *(Ibid.,* 25:41). Or again, that conclusion of the parable of the Ten Virgins: "Amen, I say unto you, I know you not" *(Ibid.,* 12). Which of us can flatter himself that the door of the banqueting hall will not be shut against him before he has found a place there? Which of us, at any rate, can boast that he will never see the sleep of death—that great sleep which must come as a surprise to us all, so infallibly, so suddenly, so soon? The world does all it can to drive away and banish these thoughts—yes, even the world which has received the Sacraments of Christ, and makes some profession of piety.

This is one of the signs by which we monks ought to be recognized. When we are asked why we have come hither, we should be able to answer truly: "To prepare ourselves for death and the judgment of God." It is this that our holy Lawgiver desires from us. He tells us so clearly both in his prologue and throughout his Rule, especially in the fourth chapter, where he puts into our hands those three instruments whose combined action should naturally produce in our souls this second kind of compunction: *To keep death daily before one's eyes. To fear the Day of Judgement. To dread hell.*\*

The third kind of compunction arises from the consideration of the numberless evils of this present life, which makes the soul feel its miserable condition here below—*ubi est.* It was this that Job felt when he cried: "The life of man upon earth is a continual warfare"† (Job 7:1); this that drew from David words such as these: *All things are vanity: every man living*‡ (Ps. 38:6); *In a desert land, and where there is no way, and no water*§ (Ps. 62:3). Thus pondering, the soul looks into herself and sees all her ruin and darkness, her rebellion and opposition to grace. Without, the spectacle is no less grievous: there is the world, which strives to drag her into its own ruin, and which hates and persecutes her so long as she perseveres in the love of

---

\* *Mortem cotidie ante oculos suspectam habere. Diem judicii timere. Gehennam expavescere.*
† *Tentatio est, vita hominis super terram.*
‡ *Universa vanitas omnis homo vivens.*
§ *In terra deserta, et invia, et inaquosa.*

Christ; there are those legions of spirits, those infernal powers, which infest the very air she breathes; there are those thousand trials by which it pleases God to prove His own. Then, in her anguish, the soul turns to Jesus; but Jesus Himself sometimes seems to sleep, and she can only cry out in her misery and terror: *Lord, save us, we perish*\* (Matt. 8:25).

From this sense of her wretchedness the soul is led naturally to desire that blessed home from which she is still absent, *ubi non est*, but whither, by God's help, she hopes one day to come. This ardent desire becomes for her a new and fourth wellspring of compunction, which is by far the most abundant, and is, moreover, the sweetest. It is the loving ardour of Magdalene, who, bent on seeking her Master, gives herself no rest until she has found Him; it is that hunger to see the face of God which brought David to feed on the bread of tears night and day (Ps. 41:4), and forced from him that cry of the exile: "Woe is me, that my sojourning is prolonged!" (Ps. 119:5).

Exalted as these sentiments may appear, St Benedict desires that his monks should make them their own. He admits to his school those Christians only who are covetous of eternal life: *Quibus ad vitam æternam gradiendi amor incumbit* (Rule, ch. 5); who are capable of aspiring after it with all the ardour of spiritual desire: *Vitam æternam omni concupiscentia spiritali desiderare*.

We should never have done if we were to repeat all the eulogies which ascetical writers have lavished on the virtue of compunction; but that which, indisputably, gives it the greatest value in our eyes is that it has been the touchstone of all that the fairest ages of the Church and the monastic orders have produced. It is this virtue which gives to the ancient formulæ of the holy liturgy their inimitable character of sweet and pen-

\* *Domine salva nos, perimus.*

etrating unction, which has inspired the most highly esteemed fruits of our own Benedictine spirituality, from the *Morals* of St Gregory, to the *Mirror for Monks* of our saintly Blosius.

Modern writers have occasionally been more learned, certainly more systematic, but they have never surpassed, even if they have equalled, the vivifying unction of the old mystical writers. There exists, still almost entirely in manuscript, an *Enchiridion* intended to initiate the novices of the congregation of Bursfeld into the daily exercises of monastic piety. It is impossible to picture to oneself without emotion the life of a monk who brings to bear upon his smallest actions that spirit of compunction which breathes in every page of this manual (due in great measure to the Abbé Jean Trithème). By giving to this virtue a chief place in our own monastic life, we shall be walking in the footsteps of our fathers, and living in conformity to our state.

Let us not fear to aspire to it; let us persevere in prayer to God for it. There is, so far as I know, no authorized prayer to obtain the gift of miracles, or visions, or other such *charismata*, but there is one in the Missal to implore the gift of tears: *pro petitione lacrimarum*. In old times the monks were accustomed to recite it each evening before leaving the church. What should hinder us from doing the like, and often repeating with them: "Almighty and merciful God, Who for Thy thirsting people didst bring forth from the rock a fountain of living water: draw, we beseech Thee, from the hardness of our hearts the waters of compunction, that we may weep for our sins, and by Thy bounty may merit to obtain their forgiveness. Amen"?

# II
# OBEDIENCE

*Et dixerunt ad Petrum, et ad reliquos apostolos:*
*Quid faciemus, viri fratres?*
"And they said to Peter and to the other apostles:
Men and brethren, what shall we do?" (Acts 2:37)

THE FIRST EFFECT of the virtue of compunction in the soul is to dispose her to do all in her power to escape all cause of terror, and to rise to whatsoever height she feels herself called by the Holy Spirit. The deceitful calm which she enjoyed when she was far from God has given place to a clear view of her perilous position. Above her head roll the thunders of Divine anger against sinners; from every corner of the horizon the winds of temptation gather their forces against her; her frail bark, injured by long carelessness and sin, seems at each moment as if it must be dashed in pieces against the rocks, or engulfed in the abyss which every movement of the waves opens beneath her; and if far, very far off, she still sees the longed-for shore of her true country, the sight only makes her present danger the more appalling. Such is the condition of the soul whom the spirit of compunction has awakened from her torpor.

Then she turns spontaneously towards Him Who has opened her eyes, for she knows that if there be any way of escaping the peril which threatens her, He alone can show it. And so she puts aside her own lights, which have been to her such miserable darkness; having now but one desire—to place her will and all its faculties at the service of her Divine Illuminator, Who alone has the knowledge, the power, and the will to save her.

"What must I do?" is the cry of every soul touched by the fear of God. It is the cry of the Jews, converted by the voice of Peter: *What shall we do, men and brethren?*\* The cry of Saul, cast to the earth on the way to Damascus: *Lord, what wilt thou have me to do?*† He had not dreamed of such a question the moment before. He was sure of what he had to do: he was going to seize the Syrian Christians, and bring them, loaded with chains, to Jerusalem. But suddenly a light strikes his eyes, and from that moment he can neither advance nor turn back; he remains in the same place, prostrate and blind, humbly asking the commands of that Jesus, Whom until then he had unwittingly persecuted. He did not arise until he had received the order to go into the town. "There," said the Lord, "it shall be told thee what thou must do"—*Et ibi dicetur tibi quid te oporteat facere.*

St Benedict supposes his disciple to be in an altogether analogous position. If this disciple has not persecuted Jesus, he is guilty none the less, since having known Him, having served His orders, he has deserted, and shown himself a coward: *thou hast strayed by the sloth of disobedience.*‡ Nevertheless, the sublime thoughts of death and judgment, heaven and hell, have awakened a salutary remorse in his soul. At the very moment when life's shadows were closing round him, when perhaps in his gloom and hardness he was about to fall asleep, a voice full of power and sweetness sounded in his ears, calling him son, and promising to lead him back into the way of life, of light and of happiness. Full of confusion and yet of hope, he does not harden his heart nor kick against the pricks; he does not obstinately close his eyes, but humbly asks with the Psalmist: "Lord, who shall dwell in Thy tabernacle, or who shall rest upon Thy holy mountain?"

---

\* *Quid faciemus, viri fratres?*
† *Domine, quid me vis facere?*
‡ *Per inoboedientiae desidiam recesseras.*

(Ps. 14:1.) It is as if he said: "What must I do to come thither?"

This disposition to prompt and unreserved obedience is, as we know, the best preparation for the monastic life; and, indeed, it is in a certain measure a condition indispensable to any religion worthy of God. When God chose the man destined to become the father of all the faithful, He began by trying his obedience, frequently demanding from him heroic sacrifices—the forsaking of his country and kindred, the immolation of Isaac. The blessings intended for all mankind are, so to speak, attached to the obedience of this one man, Abraham: *And in thy seed shall all the nations of the earth be blessed, because thou hast obeyed my voice*\* (Gen. 22:18). *Here I am, here I am,*† is the constant answer of the patriarch to every order from on high; a word sublime in its simplicity, which more than once drew tears from the Abbot of Solesmes, and made him say: "My children, *we* ought to love Abraham with all our hearts."

We have just seen the same disposition to obedience in the first converts on the day of Pentecost, and this is henceforth to be the law for all conversions, single or collective. To embrace the Christian Faith is, in the language of the Apostles, to be obedient to the faith, the truth, the Gospel. How clearly this shines out in that beautiful scene in which Cornelius presents to Peter the first fruits of the Gentiles! "And now," he says, "we are all here before thee, to hear all things which are commanded thee by the Lord"—*Nunc ergo omnes nos in conspectu tuo adsumus audire omnia, quaecumque tibi praecepta sunt a Domino* (Acts 10:33).

How is it that in these days so many souls who seem so near the truth remain to the end outside the Catholic Church, but that they try to bargain about their submission, to exact

---

\* *Benedicentur in semine tuo omnes gentes terrae, quia obedisti voci meæ*
† *Adsum, adsum.*

pledges and compensations? They do not understand that the first word of every true Christian should be the same as that of Christ at His entrance into the world—a word of entire and absolute obedience to the will of God, rightfully manifested. *Behold I come, that I should do Thy will. O my God, I have desired it, and Thy law in the midst of my heart*\* (Ps. 39:8). If this motto of obedience "is written in the beginning of the book" which contains the names of the predestinate, St Benedict could do no less than begin the code of perfection designed for his sons in like manner. *Ausculta,* that is, not simply "listen," as one might listen to purely speculative truths; but listen, adding faith to what thou hearest that thou mayest obey it. And to show that this is the true sense, he takes care to warn us immediately that his words are addressed only to those who have resolved to arm themselves with the glorious and mighty weapons of obedience: *Ad te meus sermo dirigitur, qui oboedientiæ fortissima atque praeclara arma sumis.*

This was in order to make manifest at the outset the point of view from which he, the spiritual legislator whom God gave to the West, regarded the whole monastic life; and it is assuredly the only view which takes in everything; the only one which secures to our life its unity and stability. Our great misfortune here below, the cause of the incessant troubles, the thousand painful surprises which form the tissue of human life, is, that we do not know as we ought how to reduce everything to unity. We all have within us a multitude of powers, whose aspirations are at variance with those of our neighbour, and sometimes even with one another. Originally they were perfectly subordinated to one motive power, the will, which acted in accordance with one illuminative power, the reason, itself

---

\* *Ecce venio, ut faciam voluntatem tuam. Deus meus volui, et legem tuam in medio cordis mei.*

raised by grace to an intimate union with the light of God. When sin came into the world, this equilibrium was destroyed. True, faith has rekindled the light of God in the reason; but the inward struggle, though weakened, still goes on between the diverse elements of our being. Hence, in order to re-establish unity in our lives, we must needs seek strength from without, and attach ourselves to a simple and immutable Being. This is precisely the object of obedience: steadfastly to unite our will, and by it all our faculties and actions, to God. We were right, therefore, in saying that obedience secures unity to the life of every Christian, and especially to that of the monk.

If, for instance, I enter religion drawn by the desire to sing the praises of God, I shall only be satisfied at certain moments of the day. I cannot always be in the choir, any more than I can always be meditating, or performing acts of mortification. But one thing I can always do, at every moment of the day and night, and that is *obey;* even when I sleep, I obey. Here we have the very essence and foundation of the religious life. By the side of this one, great, simple fact, all accidental differences lose more and more of their importance, as the soul draws nearer and nearer to God by charity. Experience has proved—our older brethren can bear me out— that at the beginning of the religious life the neophyte attaches great importance to one or other detail of the observance which he has embraced. The longer and the more clearly he has felt his vocation, the more is he tempted to make an ideal for himself beforehand, which it must always be painful for him to see disappointed. This, however, cannot fail to happen, since each one's ideal differs from that of his neighbour. So, here is the poor soul, every moment exposed to some shock. This thing suits him, that does not; one occupation pleases him greatly, another infinitely less. There are, perhaps, things which frighten him, and seem unbearable, and he puts a black cross against the days on which they have to be done. There is only one way of escape from all these conflicting emotions, and that is the way of obedience. Obedience participates in that sovereign independence of charity, so well described by St Paul in his Epistle to the Romans (8:35 *et seq.*). The monk also may say: "Who shall separate me from obedience? Shall change of place, of occupation, of person? No. They may expel me, like so many others, from the peaceful walls of the cloister; they may deprive me of all the consolations of the religious life; they may dispose of me in a hundred unforeseen ways; but there is one thing of which they can never rob me, and that is the happiness of obeying—*that* will go with me to death." What magnificent unity! How glorious the course of a life wholly spent in this atmosphere of obedience! From the earliest days of monasticism it has been a favourite practice to draw a parallel between a monk and a king; and certainly the contrast is a most real and striking one.

Where is the king (especially in these days of unrest and uncertainty) who can be sure that he will be wearing the crown of government to-morrow?

The monk, at least, need not fear that anyone will snatch from him that in which lies his dignity and holy pride—that is, the obedience to his Rule, which secures his kingship over himself and his passions. Let us not deceive ourselves: we shall never find happiness or true peace on earth, except in the full and joyous surrender of perfect obedience. Failing that, we may wear the monastic habit, but we shall never be monks in the true sense of the word. It is the more necessary to insist on this point, because certain modern theologians are sometimes inclined to look at religious obedience from a point of view which is not in full conformity with the doctrine contained in our Rule. Obedience appears to them rather under what we might call a negative aspect, simply as a condition indispensable to the existence and development of any religious society. The individual being drawn towards this society by one pious motive or another must, in order to belong to it, submit to the laws which govern it, and do nothing which might counteract its healthy working. It is, on the contrary, the *obedientiae bonum* (Rule, ch. 71), the excellence of obedience, that we desire before all in coming to the Abbey. The Abbot is not an administrative machine, which must be submitted to: it was precisely to seek him and his direction and authority that we came hither: *they dwell in monasteries, and desire to have an Abbot over them* \* (Rule, ch. 5).

This last word is very expressive. It is a true desire, a sort of regretful longing for Christ, such as the first Christians who were converted after Our Lord's Ascension must have felt.

When they heard the Apostles speak of their Master, how often must they have exclaimed: "Oh! if we had lived with Him, if we had received His commands directly from Himself, what a joy and what an honour it would have been for us to obey Him in the smallest things!" "What then!" replies St Paul, "know you not that Christ speaks in me?"—*loquitur in me Christus*—2 Cor. 13:3.

But it is not only in Paul nor in the other Apostles that Christ speaks. He speaks in all the pastors appointed by them and their successors, according to their place in the ecclesiastical hierarchy. Jesus says to them all: "He that heareth you heareth Me" (Luke 10:16). The Abbot, as one of these, shares most intimately and effectively in this power of commanding in the Name of Christ.

St Benedict is precise upon this point. We are bound to believe that the Abbot holds the place of Christ in the mon-

\* *In coenobiis degentes abbatem sibi praeesse desiderant.*

astery: *For he is believed to be the representative of Christ in the monastery;*\* and his very name of Abbot belongs to him only in virtue of his moral identification with Christ: *for that reason he is called by a name of His... he is called Abbot, not for any pretensions of his own, but for honour and love of Christ* †(Rule, ch. 2, 63).

The Abbot is, then, the true spiritual generator of the monastic family, and this, as has so often been remarked, is why the chapter *What kind of man the Abbot should be*‡ stands first in the Rule, after the Introduction. Any other legislator would probably have treated of the Abbot with the other officials, with the seniors, the prior, the cellarer and the rest, after matters concerning the whole community. Not so Benedict. He wished the Abbot to be the foundation-stone of the whole spiritual cloister. The first thing that is done in building a monastery is solemnly to lay the stone destined to serve as the foundation for the whole material edifice. The same thing was done in old times for the spiritual edifice: never was the swarm destined for a new foundation sent out without its first Abbot at the head. The Abbot therefore realises in himself that further title of Christ sung aforetime by the Prophets: he is the "corner-stone" of the monastery, the stone intended to insure the solidity of the whole construction, built up of souls strong and weak, innocent and penitent, noble and simple, rich and poor, learned and ignorant, all chosen by the Divine Architect, and joined together by the indestructible mortar of charity. And it is just because he has to bear the weight of the whole edifice and insure its stability that the holy Lawgiver requires so many

---

\* *Christi enim agere vices in monasterio creditur.*
† *Quando ipsius vocatur pronomine... Abbas vocetur, non sua assumptione sed honore et amore Christi.*
‡ *Qualis esse debeat Abbas.*

qualities in the Abbot. He wishes him to be "foursquare," like those strong stones of which Solomon's Temple and the Altar of Ezechiel's vision were built—that is, he must be a man of sound doctrine and virtue, mercy and justice.

Thank God, most communities in our day can congratulate themselves on this head; but even should the Abbot not be in all respects such as he ought, we must still trust and obey him. St Peter, after having said that Christ is the Foundation-Stone, laments the fate of those who will not trust in Him, but make him a "stone of stumbling" (1 Pet. 2:8), because they know not how to obey. Let us not be of this number; let us never forget that it is not man upon whom we rely, but Christ, lest we should incur the malediction of the Prophet: "Cursed is he who putteth his trust in man"—*Maledictus homo qui confidit in homine, et ponit carnem brachium suum* (Jer. 17:5). Yet Simon himself was the foundation-stone of the Church. Are there, then, two foundation-stones, Christ and Peter? No; but in Simon we have the weak and mortal man, the timid Galilean who trembles at the voice of a servant-maid, and also the proclaimer of Christ's Divinity; who was to confirm his brethren in the Faith, and to be the supreme shepherd of the sheep and the lambs. So, in every Abbot, whoever he may be, there is a *man*—fallible like us, a sinner like us, perhaps lacking more than ourselves in certain qualities. But with him, as a man, we have nothing to do—he has disappeared, hidden by the rays of light, which on the day of his election streamed upon him from the Face of Christ. It is thus transfigured that our faith must consider him. Otherwise we shall soon take scandal, even at the most perfect Abbot; for, once more, man is always man—that is to say, a being whom we cannot trust: *every man is a liar*\* (Ps. 115:2). Let us recall the scene of St Peter walking on the sea. Was the water more

\* *Omnis homo mendax.*

solid before he began to sink? Not so; but his faith in the word of Jesus had suddenly weakened, and, seeing only the winds and the waves, he became subject to the natural action of the unstable element. It is thus with ourselves and our Superiors. If we have trusted ourselves to them, it is because of the command of Christ. Sure of that command, we have set out to reach Him through them: *he walked upon the water to come to Jesus*\* (Matt. 14:29); or, as the holy Rule says (ch. 71): *Knowing that by this road of obedience they will come to God.*† But let us not forget that our safety lies in this alone—in not regarding or stopping short at the *man;* otherwise, we shall sink and perish, unless Jesus stretch forth His hand and take hold of us, saying: "O man of little faith, why didst thou doubt?" (Matt. 14:31).

There is a great mystery in this development of the power of faith in souls, in proportion as they draw nearer to God. There are monks who only do just what is necessary in order not palpably to violate the vow, or even the virtue of obedience; beyond that they do not care to rise, they are satisfied as they are. Let us beware of rashly accusing them; often it is not their fault. Perhaps God has not intended them to climb the holy ladder of obedience any higher, for here also God calls souls to many different heights (Rule, ch. 7). There are always some from whom He manifestly requires greater things, and here is one of the signs by which this vocation may be recognised. There are certain souls who, though not wanting in the natural gifts which the world esteems, sometimes find themselves a prey to a sort of grievous desolation; they who, one might suppose, would be full of expedients and great projects feel themselves deprived of all initiative. Outwardly they appear

---

\* *Ambulabat super aquam, ut veniret ad Jesum.*
† *Scientes se per hanc obedientiae viam ituros ad Deum.*

well able to direct others, and, perhaps, sometimes they have been tempted to believe this themselves; but the moment has come when they are unable to take a single step alone, even should the question only be the choice between several perfectly indifferent ways of fulfilling a single order of the Superior. Oh! how these souls should rejoice in this state, which seems so humiliating! For God never thus abandons those whom He loves, except to draw them nearer and press them more closely to His bosom. What we must do in this case is to go forward courageously into the dark night of practical faith. Without fear of being troublesome to our spiritual Father, let us show him frankly the exact state of our soul. On his side he will exhort us to seek safety in a fuller and more interior obedience. God cannot refuse to the soul that serves Him the light to guide his steps into the way of peace. Uncertainty and discouragement are never the work of God. If for a space He leaves us to them, it is that He may lovingly constrain us to seek more and more in obedience the cure of our irresolution.

The Rule and the greater part of the monastic constitutions contain very few of those minute details which might make the yoke of God's service seem heavy. The wisest founders of Benedictine congregations in our time have wished that, the great principles being once well established, all the rest should be the affair of the spirit, and governed rather by the living Rule—that is, the Abbot—than by the dead letter of any regulations whatsoever. From this it follows that if we are not careful to keep close to the Superior, we shall but seldom nourish ourselves with that bread of obedience which was the food of Jesus.

Now God, Who loves our souls, does not wish this to be; therefore He pricks our conscience, that He may compel us to utter that cry which so forcibly reminds us that we are monks—that is, men of obedience: *Quid faciemus?* What must we do at such a time, in such a situation, in these details seemingly so unimportant? *Quid faciemus?* Let this question always be accompanied by that holy charity which hopeth all things; and then, as the blessed Father says (Rule, ch. 68.), we shall be able to do "impossibilities, and even, if need be, to work miracles." The more we cease to trust in ourselves, the more shall we feel that we can do all things in Him that strengtheneth us (Phil. 4:13). In cultivating this spiritual ground, let us not be less diligent than our forefathers. Let obedience flourish amongst us as in the early days—simple, generous, heroic—and it will soon be manifest that the *strong race of Cenobites**  (Rule, ch. 1), that the race of true and great monks of former times, has not yet entirely disappeared from the Church of God.

---

* *Coenobitarum fortissimum genus.*

## III

## PENANCE

*Petrus vero ad illos: Pœnitentiam, inquit, agite.*
"And Peter said to them: Do penance" (Acts 2:38).

We have seen St Peter's hearers, touched with compunction, asking him what they were to do. Hitherto the chief of the Apostles has spoken only of the truths to be believed; he has proclaimed the mystery of Pentecost, the Resurrection of Christ, the future judgment. He passes now to the moral order. In answer to the question suggested by the inward working of the Holy Spirit, he points out what they must do in order to have part in the salvation brought by Jesus. Now, according to him, the first condition is to do penance. It is ever the same, whether set forth by the Prophets, by John the Baptist, or by Jesus Himself. "Return to the Lord" (Osee 14:3, etc.). "Bring forth worthy fruits of penance" (Matt. 3:8). "Except you do penance, you shall all perish" (Luke 13:3, 5).

What is it, then, this "doing penance"?

First of all, it is a change of soul, of thought, of opinion, μετανοεῖν. Formerly they considered things under one particular aspect, without taking any other into account; from this false and incomplete view followed actions contrary to virtue, to justice, and to their own interests. Blinded by the proud prejudices of their race, desirous of pleasing the Pharisees and the unworthy chiefs of the Synagogue, they had closed their ears to the voice of the Divine Oracles.

The wonders of all kinds wrought by Jesus under their own eyes had been unable to triumph over their evil will; some through cowardice, others through contempt or hatred: all had bartered the blood of the Galilean. At last, however, light has broken in upon them, and they see their guilt. But the evil is done, beyond repair. Man may take life, but he cannot give it back; that is in the power of God alone, *the Lord killeth and maketh alive*\* (1 Kings 2:6). Is there, then, no hope?

Yes; in revenging on ourselves the treatment inflicted on the Son of God.

We must doom to death everything in ourselves which has been the cause of His death. Death, then, to those rash and unjust judgments, death to the risings of pride, death to those movements of passion, death to everything which might be for us an occasion of revolt against God. And what death, do you ask? The same death by which we slew the Lord Jesus. We crucified Him, therefore that which nailed Him to the Cross must be crucified. We must crucify that miserable and accursed part of our nature, which St Paul calls the old man— *our old man is crucified with him*† (Rom. 6:6), with its vices and concupiscences, with what the same Apostle does not hesitate at the risk of covering us with just confusion, to call "our members which are upon the earth"—*Mortify therefore your members which are upon the earth; fornication, uncleanness, lust, evil concupiscence, and covetousness*‡ (Col. 3:5).

But this is only the negative side of penance. We have said that it consists in a change of soul; consequently, it not only kills the old man within us, but gives life to and develops the new.

---

\* *Dominus mortificat et vivificat.*
† *Vetus homo noster simul crucifixus est.*
‡ *Mortificate ergo membra vestra, quae sunt super terram: fornicationem, immunditiam, libidinem, concupiscentiam malam, et avaritiam.*

Since death was conquered by life, nothing, by the dispensation of God, has ever died, except to render distinct service to the interests of life. Christ was thenceforward the great Model, the universal Type. Now, Christ died only to rise again. Wheresoever the efficacy of the Divine Remedy which streamed forth on Calvary has extended, there has been the work of death and the work of life. The work of death to destroy and consume all the fruits of sin within us; the work of life to set free and expand to its utmost capacity everything in our being capable of receiving grace and glory. This work may be, as yet, hidden with Christ *(Ibid.,* 3), but it is none the less real; it seems so, only because Christ, our Life, has not yet appeared. But when He shall again manifest Himself we shall be like Him, sons of God, living to the full the life of God which has become our life. Let us never forget that this is the meaning of our baptism. It is not a mere oratorical comparison, an ingenious combination of thoughts or words. Once more, St Paul never considers Christianity otherwise than under this double aspect of death and life working in our souls—that is to say, under the aspect of penance. And this idea was so familiar to the first Christians, that with them, to receive baptism and to do penance were synonymous terms, as we see clearly from the documents of the primitive Church.

How is it that such an elementary notion has been almost completely obliterated from the minds of so many Christians of our day? More in some lands than in others, for the contagion of ideas subversive of the supernatural order has not penetrated everywhere to the same extent. However, there is certainly one thing that characterises the world in which we were brought up, and whose atmosphere we have all breathed more or less: and that is the denial in theory, and even more in practice, of original sin and its consequences. This is how we must explain the daily increasing success of those principles of pretended liberty, which, as those around us understand them, suppose natures exempt from decadence, capable from their earliest years of discerning and following the right way without any sort of violence, or constraint, or even of effectual help. To this also must be attributed the absolute lack of intelligence, even in certain souls naturally religious, about what tends to the reformation of man, as God desires it. They admit the other practices of the Christian life, up to a certain point; but of this austere law of penance they understand nothing, and run their heads blindly against the rampart of mortification. Sad to say, this naturalistic point of view is gaining ground all over the world, even invading the borders of Catholicism at the risk of endangering its success. Whence comes it, that men of God sometimes seem mistrustful of apparent conquests of the Church in certain regions, but that this element of mortification, without which it is impossible to conceive of any stability in the spiritual life, so seldom receives its rightful place?

Our holy Father Benedict had quite another conception of Christ and His work. He hides from us none of the difficulties which we shall encounter on our way to the mountain of God, warning us from the outset that it will be his duty to prescribe anything whatsoever that may help in the amendment of our vices—*Dictante aequitatis ratione, propter emendationem vitiorum* (Rule, Prologue). The beginnings, especially, will be painful, and he wishes that everyone coming to the monastery with the intention of remaining should be told this. He must be spared nothing, but be warned beforehand of all the hard and painful things he will have to bear (Rule, ch. 58). And when the time comes for him to bind himself before God and his brethren by irrevocable vows, one of his three promises will be to labour for the conversion of his manners. From this moment until death his whole life can be summed up in this one word: "To share, by patience, in the sufferings of Christ"—*Passionibus Christi per patientiam participemus.* Is not this, in substance, the programme of the penitential and mortified life which St Paul required of the first Christians?

As to the exact practices corresponding to this programme, our holy Lawgiver is, as we know, singularly moderate. We might say, without too much exaggeration, that the régime which he assigned to his monks was, in the main, that to which numbers of good Christians of his time submitted. In fact, we need only glance at certain documents witnessing to the discipline of the sixth century—for example, the Homilies of St Cæsarius of Arles—to see that more was required of simple lay folk than our blessed Father imposed on his disciples. If we consult other monastic codes, earlier and later than St Benedict's, such as the Rules of Irish origin—that of St Columban, for instance—what shall we see? We all know the place which these assign to those disciplinary measures whose rigour terrifies our modern weakness. Doubtless God had His own designs in inspiring our Patriarch with greater discretion. It is certain that if Western Monachism had entrenched itself in the austere practices of an asceticism, exaggerated or cultivated for its own sake, it would never have been so widespread nor, consequently, so powerful; it would never have exercised that great civilizing influence over Christian society which all men recognise today.

Nevertheless, the monk should always be, as someone has said, "the pinnacle of the Church's sanctity" (Littré, *Etudes sur les Barbares et le moyen âge,* p. 141). St Benedict, when he refrained from giving his sons a whole official apparatus of asceticism, never intended to deprive them of the help towards attaining the highest degrees of the Christian life, which is found in the heroic exercises of penance. Many before him had made the sum of Christian asceticism to consist chiefly of exterior practices; and hence arose those types of sanctity which, especially in the East, were too exaggerated and sometimes too singular to be proposed as models for that just moderation, that wise balance, which the true understanding of Christianity implies.

Benedict sought his inspiration elsewhere. Without neglecting anything of the heritage of practical wisdom left him by his predecessors, he recalled that great principle, that "God is a Spirit, and those who adore Him, must adore Him in spirit and in truth." In a religion founded on so spiritual a basis it is evident that exercises of corporal mortification ought not entirely or even chiefly to absorb our efforts. It is the inward reform, through faith and charity, at which we must aim before all else. There is no doubt that in this respect St Augustine exercised a great influence over Western Monachism, and especially over our holy Lawgiver, as much by the breadth of his teaching as by the example of his life. God would seem to have chosen this incomparable man that through him He might manifest this truth, that the first thing which we must seek is love—*In the first place, to love the Lord God*\* (Rule, ch. 4.)—and that, if it is good and lawful to seek this love in penance, it is still better and more attractive to great souls to make love their executioner by seeking penance in love. St Benedict lived at the very time when the Roman Church was translating this important doctrine into those august formulæ which delight us to this day, especially during the Lenten fast. Hence, it follows that according to him the monk's true cross is interior, it is the renunciation of his own will, which is obedience. All the rest must flow from and be controlled by this. Similarly, when the Blessed Father, laying aside his usual reserve, exhorts his sons to add during Lent some acts of corporal mortification to their usual exercises, he is careful to add that this must only be done with the Abbot's consent; thus

\* *In primis Dominum Deum diligere.*

giving us to understand that obedience is the very first and the most indispensable mortification. This is the reason that while he shows a liberality which for his time might seem to us surprising in questions of eating and drinking, conversation and sleep, he is rigorous towards murmuring. It is because murmuring is the surest mark of an unmortified soul, and directly opposed to that holy indifference, to that joyous alacrity of the truly obedient monk, that the master never loses an occasion of denouncing it to his disciples as a danger to be avoided before all and above all.

Thus, the monk who applies himself with all his heart to the perfect acquisition of obedience will necessarily be mortified and penitent. However, the blessed Father in no wise forbids the way of holy austerity to those of his sons whom grace calls to it. He wishes, on the contrary, that there should be room in his monasteries for the strong who desire to do more—*ut sit et fortes quod cupiant* (Rule, ch. 64.)—for we cannot imagine that he would have shown such indulgence to the weak, unless he had assured this liberty to the strong.

There must be in the Church those great examples of exterior penance, that all may see the reality of the transformation which Christianity effects in the soul. Indeed, for very many these mortifications are the only means of attaining that degree of interior purification to which God calls them.

If, in fact, according to the scholastic axiom, nothing exists in the intellect which has not first passed through the senses, it is true also, up to a certain point, that interior mortification can hardly attain its normal development without some courageous attempts at bodily mortification. We have already said the same thing with regard to exterior recollection, which the blessed Father calls the last step of the ladder of humility, but which, in its beginnings, is indispensable to anyone who wishes to climb even the first step.

It is especially in the first days of their conversion that God inspires souls with this generous ardour for exterior mortifications. Doubtless this feeling is often, if not always, mingled with a certain natural element, which prevents more advanced souls from being mistaken as to its real value. Such as it is, however, it is most surely a gift of God; and to set it aside, or altogether to thwart it, would be a grievous error, and would come very near to what St Paul calls "extinguishing the Spirit" (1 Thess. 5:19). Let our Superiors regulate its manifestations as they will, but let us always cover this sacred fire with the ashes of humility, so that we may find it again in due time. Let us not fail to stir it up from time to time, especially in penitential seasons, such as Lent, or the vigils of great feasts, by asking our Superior's leave to practise such or such acts of penance. This is already an honoured practice amongst us, and is in accordance with the spirit of the holy Rule. But do not let us content ourselves with what is official: the soul which has that good zeal of which the blessed Father speaks (Rule, ch. 72.) will often feel drawn in the course of the year to something more spontaneous. Of a surety, God never draws near to a soul which He desires to unite to Himself in a more intimate manner without asking of it that "living sacrifice, holy, pleasing to God" (Rom. 12:1), which, the Apostle tells us, is the immolation of our own body.

Our first duty when God has thus spoken to the soul of one of our brethren, and when the Superior has given his consent, is to do nothing which may impede the liberty of the Divine action, but to uphold it with supreme respect. I say *uphold*, because it is only too natural in a community that outward signs of progress in others should cause a certain jealousy and sadness in souls who do not feel themselves so far advanced, and who are not yet sufficiently rooted in charity to understand that one of the most marvellous and most assured results of this virtue is to hold all goods in common amongst those who truly love one another in God. So it happens that we not infrequently see the desire of corresponding to grace stifled in certain souls by their fear of appearing to wish to undertake more than others. This sudden arresting of the spiritual flight, in an atmosphere meant to advance it by ensuring and directing its freedom, is most deplorable, and utterly contrary to the true monastic spirit. There seems no need to dwell further on this point, except to remind ourselves that we must be on our guard against the first movements of Nature. Remember the large-hearted and beautiful teaching of St Paul in the fourteenth chapter of his Epistle to the Romans: "Let not him that eateth despise him that eateth not: and he that eateth not, let him not judge him that eateth. Let every man act according to his conviction, and in the Lord's sight. He that eateth, let him eat in the Lord's sight, and he that eateth not, to the Lord let him abstain. For none of us liveth to himself, and no man dieth to himself. For whether we live, we live unto the Lord; or whether we die, we die unto the Lord." Whether we live, therefore, or die, we belong to the Lord by holy obedience, which inspires all our actions. How, after this, can we judge our brother, who is another man's servant?

And over and above these special inspirations we shall find in the holy Rule a continual invitation to mortify ourselves, if we thoroughly grasp one of its characteristic features; I mean that invariable habit of setting beside the smallest fault its salutary remedy of satisfaction.

Is it possible for men who continually submit to such satisfactions for some light infringement of the Rule—an involuntary negligence, the breaking of some object, inexactitude in the Office—is it possible for them to think lightly of the obligation of satisfying Divine justice for their interior and daily faults; above all, for those graver and more numerous, which, perhaps, they come to the monastery to expiate? Even if, by God's grace, they offend Him less than others, will not the sight of that ocean of sin around them, whose waves once pressed with all their weight upon the head of the dear and sacred Victim, inspire them with something of that zeal which filled the prophet Elias, for the Lord God of hosts (3 Kings 19:10)? And without attempting to pose as victims, will they not at least rejoice to associate themselves with the heroic efforts of so many souls who seek to repair the outrages committed against the Divine Majesty, to impetrate His mercy for the immeasurable guilt of the world? Will they not gladly make trial of some thorns of that blood-stained crown, the only one which their Spouse willed to know on earth?

Certainly none of this is pleasing to nature. But let us not forget the words of our blessed Father (Prologue, ch. 7.): The heart will speedily be enlarged by the beneficent action of the spirit of penance, and at last love will reign so absolutely as to cast out all other influence. Thank God, we have daily before our eyes touching examples of this; therefore we need not fear that the perpetual cry of cowardly souls in all times, that our weakened constitutions are unable to bear the penances of former days, will easily find favour amongst us. That we are weaker is an indisputable fact; and the Church, in her discretion, has taken this into account, and has mitigated to a considerable extent the rigour of primitive discipline. But it is none the less true that God, even in our own day, continues to inspire chosen souls with an equal ardour for the holy austerities of a life of penance; and that the religious life would lose almost all its lustre if it were to be modified in this respect, to suit the current opinion of our times. That venerable servant of God, Mother Margaret Hallahan, who was so penetrated with the Benedictine spirit, thought and expressed this. "In her instructions, no less than by her example," says her biographer, "she strongly protested against that false and effeminate spirituality of our time, which professes to sanctify the spirit without mortifying the flesh." And upon this subject she pronounced these weighty words: "I believe that the cause of all the weakness and insubordination which we meet with today amongst religious is the neglect and rejection of exterior penance."

## IV
## BAPTISM AND PROFESSION

*Et baptizetur unusquisque vestrum ... in remissionem peccatorum.*
"Do penance, and be baptized every one of you,
for the remission of your sins" (Acts 2:38).

PENANCE—THAT IS TO SAY, the power to change his interior dispositions—is a great means of salvation for man. The angels do not possess it, and this is why having once turned towards evil, the proud spirits at once became fixed in it, without the power of ever again turning to their Creator. Man, on the contrary, from the very fact of his natural inferiority, is never so fixed in evil whilst on earth but that he may hope, by the help of Divine mercy, to regain all, even when everything seems lost.

But, again, this very facility of repentance is in itself a real danger. It is to be feared that man, who repents so quickly, may as easily repent of good as of evil; and daily experience proves that this fear is but too well founded. To prevent these deplorable relapses among His faithful children, Christ permits them to become part of His mystical body only after submitting to a mysterious initiation, the remembrance and efficacy of which would make backsliding and apostasy almost impossible. The name of this initiation is the Sacrament of Baptism; and this is why St Peter, having exhorted his hearers to do penance, immediately counsels them to fix themselves firmly and for ever in their new dispositions by receiving Baptism, promising them that thus their sins would be remitted—*and be baptized every one of you for the remission of your sins*\*.

\* *Et baptizetur unusquisque vestrum in remissionem peccatorum.*

In like manner, the monk, before he can be admitted into the monastic family, must submit to a corresponding initiation—that of holy Profession—which shall for ever establish him in the religious life. Here we will say a few words on the many analogies between this monastic Profession and Christian Baptism; we shall then see how the expiatory value of profession may, in a certain sense, be likened to that of Baptism.

Christian Baptism exacts in the first place a longer or shorter period of preparation—the catechumenate. In this stage the candidates undergo exorcisms, and listen to the catechizing given by the Bishop, or by his substitute. Towards the end of this time of probation take place the *traditio legis christianae*—handing over of the Christian law—and the scrutiny by which must be decided the admission of the neophyte to Baptism.

The aspirant to the monastic Profession must also pass through a kind of catechumenate; this is the novitiate—that period of twelve months during which he must patiently submit to all the tests and corrections to which the Abbot or his representative may think fit to subject him. What are these little tests but so many forms of imprecation—true exorcisms, meant to extinguish all claims of the Evil One over the soul which desires to consecrate itself entirely to God? Let us call to mind those two incidents in the life of our blessed Father: the stroke of the rod which freed the slothful monk from the influence of the little black imp, and the blow which drove the evil spirit out of the body of the good old Brother. Reprimands, hard words, and penances inflicted by the Novice-Master are so many strokes of the rod, so many blows, aimed at our enemy. Let him do what he will with us.

When the Church is about to consecrate anything to God, whether it be water, or salt, a bell, or a place of prayer, she begins by exorcism, by the complete expulsion of the demon;

she can do no less when it is a question of perfectly restoring to her service the rational creature who furnished Satan with the occasion of exercising his empire over the world.

Another of our aspirants' duties is to pay devout heed to the special and more frequent instructions given them during the year of novitiate. They must come out from it bearing in their hearts that *leaven of divine justice*\* of which the holy Rule speaks (ch. 2.), and which should impart a heavenly fragrance to every action of their monastic career. They must be deeply imbued with the true Christian spirit, so little understood by the world today; they must have a holy love and enthusiasm for the beauty of their vocation, and omit nothing which may enable them to follow it in all its fulness.

Then towards the end of their probation, if they are found faithful, comes the "scrutiny" which decides their admission into the family of God; and then it is that for the last time, and with greater solemnity, the holy Rule is offered to them: that Rule which they have read, have thrice heard explained, and which is to be henceforward the law of their spiritual warfare—*Behold the law under which you wish to serve.*†

At last, all being prepared, comes the monk's Profession. This august rite has doubtless varied in different times and countries, and even at the present day it varies in different congregations and monasteries. Nevertheless, we everywhere find the four elements corresponding to the four principal parts of the ritual of Baptism—renunciation, profession of faith, mystical death, and, finally, the delivery of the emblems of the new life.

The ceremony of Baptism opens with a threefold renunciation: "Dost thou renounce Satan?" asks the priest of the

---
\* *Fermentum divinae justitiae.*
† *Ecce lex, sub qua militare vis.*

neophyte. "I renounce him." "And all his works?" "I renounce them." "And all his pomps?" "I renounce them."

Such, also, is the import of the questions which the Abbot puts to the novice at the end of the address expressly intended to remind him that his Profession will be to him as a second Baptism. The Abbot asks him: "Will you renounce the world and its pomps?" "I will." "Will you renounce even the love of your kindred, in so far as it may be opposed to the love due to Jesus Christ?" "I will." "Will you renounce your own will, to submit yourself to the yoke of obedience?" "I will." This is the monk's threefold renunciation—a renunciation which supports, completes, and perfects that which was made in Baptism.

But this is only the negative side of the great act about to be accomplished. The aspirant to Baptism, after having renounced Satan, and just as he is about to descend into the font, is required to profess his adherence to Christ; which he does by repeating aloud the Creed, the profession of the Christian faith.

Such, also, is the second act of our aspirant to the monastic life. After having renounced the pomps of the world, the inordinate love of kindred, and his own will, he also pronounces his formula of practical faith—his Profession—which binds him for ever to Christ by a threefold promise, corresponding to the threefold renunciation: stability, which binds him to his post in spite of all the ties of family and affection which might draw him back to the world; conversion of manners, which obliges him to free himself more and more from the spirit and maxims of the age; and, lastly, obedience, which in future must take the place occupied by self-will in the past.

This Profession is followed, according to the best monastic traditions, by a mysterious scene, equivalent to the immersion of the neophyte in the baptismal font. St Paul has himself explained the symbolism of this immersion which makes the faithful partakers of Christ's death and burial—*For we are buried together with Him by baptism into death*\* (Rom. 6:4). As the initiated disappears beneath the water, the minister of God pronounces the Sacramental formula: "I baptize thee in the Name of the Father, and of the Son, and of the Holy Ghost."

In like manner, according to the monastic ceremonial, when the newly professed has pronounced the formula of his vows, he immediately puts himself as it were into a state of death, prostrating himself at full length on the floor of the sanctuary. And it is still further to accentuate this idea of death and burial, that for many centuries those mournful solemnities—the funeral pall, the tapers, and the tolling of the bell—have been in use; and although, sometimes, they may have been taken out of their original setting, the underlying idea remains the same. During this prostration of the newly professed, the Abbot recites over him those four solemn prayers, which, as the old writers say, "make the monk"—*ad faciendum monachum*—and which, being addressed successively to the three Persons of the august Trinity, are in some sort a development of that sacred formula to which we are indebted for our regeneration.

But, as we have said before, nothing dies that belongs to God, save to enter on a new and better life. This new life is the life of Christ. This is what St Paul teaches in continuing his explanation of the rite of Baptism. "All you," he says, "who have been baptized into Christ, have put on Christ" (Gal. 3:27). It is as though he said: Let not that Divine life which you have received with the waters of the sacred fountain cease to spring up in you, from you, and over you. Keep it, by the habitual communion of your spirit and life with Christ's, as the ordinary garment which shows what you are, your rank and condition in life.

\* *Consepulti enim sumus cum Christo per baptismum in mortem.*

This is the origin of that white robe given to the neophyte on leaving the font, to remind him that the grace of Baptism has made him "another Christ." But this symbol did not suffice; the same idea was reproduced under many forms. Christ is the Messiah, the Lord's Anointed; Christ is also the Head of mankind—*the head of every man is Christ*\* (1 Cor. 2:3).

To express this doctrine, the head of the newly baptized is anointed with perfumed oil—the chrism. Again, Christ is King; and, as king, He has His emblem, His sign, which all who fight under Him must bear. This is the cross which the priest traces on the brow of each neophyte as he signs him with the "chrism of salvation" and bids him go in peace. Lastly, Christ is the Light, and so a lighted taper is put into the hand of the newly baptized. And, to show that the spiritual clothing is not only exterior, like the habit, behold the seal of all these mysteries: the Sacrament of the Body and Blood of Christ, which instils itself into the very marrow of our being, there to work that marvellous interpenetration, that supreme consummation, from which our Lord, in His love for us, did not shrink.

All this symbolic clothing has its parallel on the day of our Profession—more austere, no doubt, but not less significant. Nothing is wanting. If, in the colour of the distinguishing habit which is put upon us at this solemn moment, black has replaced the dazzling whiteness of the Paschal tunic, it is to teach us that this second Baptism is more toilsome than the first; a baptism of penance, in which the state of death will end only with the illusive and deceptive life which we lead on earth. The unction of joy and peace of our first Baptism is represented to us by the fraternal embrace, during which we sing of the union of hearts which the Lord hath blest; that union which

\* *Omnis viri caput Christus est.*

the Psalmist compares to the sweet perfume which ran down from the head of Aaron to the border of his garment.

As to the signing with the cross, it formed part of the monastic initiation in the East from the earliest times. In the West, the very shape of the cowl is a sufficient symbol of the Lord's Cross; so much so, that the taking of the habit by the newly professed was expressed briefly by this formula: *Dominicae cruci dedicari*—to be dedicated, vowed, consecrated to the Cross of the Lord.

The lighted taper, also, is a part of the monastic ritual of the East. With us it is touchingly and expressively supplied by the call of the deacon to the new brother, when he is about to draw near to Christ, the Light, and from Him to "trim" the lamp of his heart—*Arise you who sleep… and Christ will illuminate you*\* *(Cf.* Eph. 5:14*).* Was it not this aspect of the Holy Eucharist which dictated to the Primitive Church, as her habitual chant of Communion, that beautiful thirty-third Psalm, which says: "Come ye to Him, and be enlightened" —*Accedite ad eum, et illuminamini.*

One last feature will complete the analogy between the ceremonial of Baptism and that of monastic Profession. The neophyte does not return to his ordinary life directly after his Baptism. For a certain number of days he wears his white tunic, assists at the Holy Mysteries, diligently frequents the House of God, having a place apart in the assembly of the Christian community. He does not enter the ordinary ranks of the faithful until he has put off his neophyte's garment on the Saturday, *in albis*. Our fathers have imitated closely with respect to the young professed monks the directions of the Church for her new recruits. In most of our monasteries the monk, for a few days after his Profession, had constantly to wear the cowl with

---

\* *Surge, qui dormis… et illuminabit te Christus.*

which the Abbot had clothed him, and to observe absolute silence. It was even the custom to sew up the opening at the front of the hood in such a way that it could not be taken off by night or day, and in some abbeys this custom still continues. At last, when these days were ended, there took place, during the conventual Mass, the *apertio oris*—the opening of the mouth—of the newly professed, who went up to the altar to receive Holy Communion. We know that two at least of these ancient customs have been retained—the habitual wearing of the cowl for the three days following Profession, and the opening of the mouth, at the Chapter, on the morning of the fourth day.

We should be mistaken if we saw only an interesting archaeological fact in this series of remarkable coincidences. They express a great and solid doctrine—namely, that in the mind of ecclesiastical tradition our Profession is truly a second Baptism which, like the first, remits all the penalty due to sin.

Lastly, a theologian of our Order has been at pains to bring together the authorities on which this doctrine rests. And, indeed, there are few propositions, outside the truths of faith properly so called, which rest on such solid foundations. These are, in the first place, the Fathers of the Church, who, from St Jerome to St Bernard, are unanimous in comparing the monastic Profession sometimes to Baptism, sometimes to Martyrdom, which is itself only a baptism of blood. Commentators on the Rule, great monastic synods, the liturgy of divers religious institutes, echo the teaching of tradition. St Thomas, who is followed by the whole medieval school, also pronounces in favour of the same doctrine. Canon Law itself officially sanctions it; whilst mystical writers make it the point of departure of their considerations on the excellence of the religious state.

All this, doubtless, is well calculated to inspire us with a high idea of this venerable rite, at which we can never assist without fresh emotion. Let those, above all, who are preparing with all the fervour of their soul to pronounce their holy vows, profit by this teaching. And let us who have already accomplished this great act, and who sometimes fear that we have not profited by it as we should, take courage by the remembrance of this solidly established doctrine—that the power of remitting all the penalty due to sin is attached, not to the act of Profession only, but even to its simple renewal, whether made in public or in private with the interior dispositions which are presupposed by the formula of the holy vows. This opinion, already known to us through the pages of those two great Saxon nuns of the thirteenth century, Gertrude and Mechtild, has since been supported by an imposing array of theologians, such as St Bernardine of Sienna, Denys the Carthusian, the Doctors of Salamanca, St Alphonsus, and, still more recently, the venerable founder of Beuron, Abbot Maurus Wolter.

Without insisting on the intrinsic reasons for attaching weight to these theologians, there is enough to inspire us with a true devotion to this exercise of the renewal of vows, which in many congregations is performed officially once a year, but which every fervent Religious will love to reiterate every day of his monastic career.

We have in our breviary, at the end of the Act of Thanksgiving after Mass, a formula—richly indulgenced by the Church—composed by the learned Haeften, Prior of Afflighem. Let us use it as often as our devotion prompts us.

To complete the above summary of the meaning and value of holy Profession, it is necessary to remark that it does not only share in the satisfactory virtue of Baptism. It has another effect—that of enhancing the dignity and supernatural merit of our smallest actions. We shall see this if we borrow some comparisons from St Anselm's delightful colloquies on the monastic life. I know that they have done good to more than one weak and hesitating soul, and they cannot but confirm others in the fervour and joy of their vocation.

Anselm, then, compares the professed monk and the secular to two men, each of whom has on his land a tree bearing a large crop of excellent fruit. Both seek their common lord, desiring to render him an act of homage. The latter says: "Lord, I have a tree in my field which bears beautiful fruit. I promise to gather, and to come and offer you a certain quantity each year." The former approaches, saying: "Lord, I also have a tree which bears abundant fruit; but I love you and respect your dignity so greatly that I should be ashamed to offer you only some of its produce; deign to accept, therefore, the tree itself. From henceforth I give it up to your steward. Let him cultivate it, and gather all the fruit." Which of these two men makes the most acceptable offering? Certainly the one who offers the whole tree. "Well," says the Saint, "it is exactly the same with the monk and the secular. Both have within them by nature and by grace a tree capable of bearing magnificent fruit for God. But what does the secular do? He offers to the Lord his good actions only, reserving for himself the will from which they proceed. The monk, on the contrary, in his undivided love for his Lord, throws himself at his feet, and says: 'Take all—the fruit and the tree itself, the good actions and the will. All henceforward to be dependent on your steward, the Abbot, who is charged to govern your domain.' Thus," concludes the Saint, "there is no doubt but that the good actions of a Religious are, by the mere fact of his Profession, far more agreeable to God than the same actions offered by a secular" (St Anselm, *De Similitudinibus*, 84; Migne, 159, 655).

There remains, however, one fear. All this is very well, it may be urged, so long as the monk remains faithful to the fervour of his vocation; but a day may come when this fervour grows cold and discipline hateful. Saint Anselm says this in no way matters, provided he never voluntarily breaks the ties by which he is bound. The monk, in fact, is like a sick man whose body is full of evil humours. The physicians declare that unless he will submit to a painful operation he must die. The patient is told of the gravity of his state, and does not hesitate to consent to the treatment; but as he has good reason not to trust himself, he begs that he may be securely bound until the operation is over. This is done. But scarcely has the sick man felt the steel than he becomes furious—shrieking out, declaring that he is not really ill, begging the surgeons to stop, and uttering terrible threats if they do not immediately unloose him. But it is only his first request that must be considered; and in spite of his protests and his cries of pain, the surgeons remain firm and finish the operation. Very soon the sick man, freed from the poison which threatened his life, regains his full strength, and is the first to thank those who did not give in to the entreaties made in a moment of weakness. "What, then," says the Saint; "was the operation of no use because he was unnerved for an instant under the surgeon's knife? This sick man is none other than he who, wishing to be cured of his vices, binds himself by the threefold vow of stability, conversion of manners, and obedience. He may afterwards feel tempted to rebel against his spiritual physicians; he may at times be refractory and ill-humoured, and protest that there is nothing wrong with his soul; but, provided he does not go so far as himself to loose his bonds, there need be no fear as to the final result. Completely cured of the malady which was paralyzing his supernatural life, he will be the first to congratulate himself on having been bound by his own free will; and so his subsequent folly will not be a hindrance to the good for which he hoped from the holy promises made at his Profession" (*Ibid.*, 80).

Let us rejoice, then, in this salutary constraint, which protects us against ourselves, and confirms us in that state of penance, to which, following the counsel of the Apostle, we have pledged ourselves. Let us thank God for having put at the disposal of those whom He loves this second Baptism, which restores and secures to so many of the faithful the sublime prerogatives of the first. Both are our glory and our joy; and each deserves our eternal gratitude, as the Church yearly reminds us in the Introit for Whitsun Tuesday: *Accipite jucunditatem gloriae vestrae, gratias agentes Deo, qui vos ad coelestia regna vocavit*—Receive the joy of your glory, giving thanks to God, Who hath called you to a heavenly kingdom.

# V
# THE APOSTOLIC LIFE

*Erant autem perseverantes in doctrina apostolorum.*
"And they were persevering in the doctrine of the Apostles"
(Acts 2:42).

WE ENTER NOW upon a new phase in the narrative of the Acts. We have seen St Peter's hearers touched with compunction, asking what they must do. St Peter has replied: "Do penance, and be baptized"; and three thousand men have immediately followed his counsel. It is the life of these new recruits, these first-fruits of the new-born Church, that St Luke is now going to describe to us; and tradition, in conformity with the text I have just quoted, has given to it the name of the Apostolic Life. At the present day we generally apply this term to those who exercise the ministry of preaching, whether in their own country or in foreign missions. In the first twelve centuries the word "apostolic" was understood in a totally different sense. An Apostolic man—*vir apostolicus*—was a man leading the life of the Apostles and their immediate successors. The apostolic life was the life of those who strove to imitate the conduct of the first Christians, and was *par excellence*, and, speaking generally, the monastic life. This is the particular doctrine developed in the little work: *De vita vere Apostolica* (Migne P. L. 170, 611-664) attributed to the venerable Abbot Rupert of Deutz.

*A propos* of the new Orders which, since the end of the eleventh century, had begun to spring up, the author asks himself if the apostolic life consisted, as some maintained, in baptising, preaching, and working miracles. After having shown the absurd consequences of such a doctrine, he demonstrates, on the authority of Cassian, that the true apostolic life is none other than that of the first Christians, which, since it could not be practised with the same fervour by the ever-increasing multitude of the baptised, ended by finding refuge in a narrow circle of chosen souls, eager to remain faithful to the ideal taught and practised by the Apostles. Those chosen souls were the first monks.

The Abbot's language was not inspired by mere *esprit de corps*. St Augustine and St Jerome know no other, and St Benedict himself, in his Rule, teaches us the same doctrine, often sending us back to the life of the first Christians, as for example, when speaking of the distribution of goods amongst the brethren (Rule, ch. 34), or commanding them to avoid—in the sale of their goods—the frauds committed by Ananias and Sapphira in the earliest days of the Church (Rule, ch. 57), or when, finally, he expressly declares that we are never more truly monks than when imitating the manner of life of our fathers in the faith, and of the Apostles themselves—*Then they are truly monks when they live by the labour of their hands, like our fathers and the Apostles*\* (Rule, ch. 48). This, then, is our model—the life of the first Christians; the life which sprang up with the beginning of the Church, under the twofold influence of Apostolic precept and example. And, truly, we might seek in vain for a better reason for making our boast in God that we are monks. We are sometimes accused of being behind the times, of stopping short at the Middle Ages, and making the life of the Church end with them, at the risk of reducing ourselves to the condition of relics—venerable, if you will, and

---

\* *Tunc vere monachi sunt, si labore manuum suarum vivunt sicut et patres nostri et apostoli.*

magnificently shrined, but relics still—dried up and seemingly lifeless, in the midst of the Christian society of our days. No; we have no intention of going back to the Middle Ages, or to anything that may be superannuated in their institutions. Neither do we think that the Church's life ends at such or such a page of history. But we know that that life was never richer or more abundant than at the beginning, while the Earth was still warm with the Blood shed upon Calvary. What we believe is that the Apostles really received "the first-fruits of the Spirit"— that is (according to the explanation of the Gloss, confirmed by St Thomas), before, and more abundantly than others—*et tempore prius, et ceteris abundantius*. Our one ambition is to follow as closely as possible the manner of life which they inaugurated in the Church, to keep the fulness of their spirit, in spite of the minimising of truth and the decline of charity, which the centuries have brought. We wish to get near to the trunk of the tree, to remain closely united to it, to live by its robust fulness of life. Others, seeing the branches, with their flowers and fruits, may imagine that all the life is there, where the action of the sap is most visible; but what would all this be without the trunk whose fibres communicate their own abundant life to all the rest?

Our root is Christ, whom we address under this title in the Advent prayer: *O radix Jesse*; and whom Isaias saw springing out of the earth—*as a root out of a thirsty ground*\*(Isa. 53:2)—that is, from the virginal womb of Mary. The trunk which connects all the rest immediately with the root is the Apostolic Succession, which God has chosen to preserve the Christian sap to the end of time in its pristine strength and richness. The foliage and the fruit change from year to year—even the smaller branches may disappear through a thousand accidents;

\* *Sicut radix de terra sitienti.*

but as long as the tree lives the main stem will keep its vitality. Now, the monks have always been looked upon as belonging to the main stem of the Church, so that it has been said: "The monk and the oak are eternal" (Lacordaire, *Mémoire pour le Rétablissement des Frères-Prêcheurs*, p.68), a phenomenon eloquently expressed in the device of our venerable Abbey of Monte Cassino: *Having been cut down, it flourishes*\*.

From all this there arise for us many important obligations. If we observe the trunk of any tree whatsoever, we shall discover three distinctive qualities. The first is Unity; the rest of the tree, covered with a thousand superfluous accessories, branches out in all directions; the trunk alone remains in its majestic unity. Nevertheless, this unity is by no means isolation; it is the channel of all the life circulating to the utmost extremity of the tree; this is what in the Church we call Catholicity. Finally, there is a third quality—strength, that vigour which in the trunk only increases with years, whilst the branches become ever more frail and tender.

These three distinctive notes must characterise all those who are called to perpetuate the Apostolic life in the Church: unity, by their close union with the Roman See; the fulness of Catholic life, by having at heart the worldwide interests of the Church; above all, attachment to the great traditions of primitive sanctity, in opposition to the degeneracy of modern times.

First, then, the monk must live in intimate union with the Holy See. This is self-evident. Let us look back to the beginnings of the Church, when the unity of the faithful was as great as their number was small. What was then the bond and centre of unity, but Peter?

It is Peter who presides at the election of Matthias, who makes the first converts among the Jewish people, as he will

---

\* *Succisa virescit.*

receive also into the Church the first-fruits of the Gentiles. It is at Peter's feet that the faithful lay the price of their lands and houses; it is he who visits Saul immediately after his conversion. It is Peter, the head, whom we see going "from town to town to visit the saints." The day will come when Peter will be thrown into prison by Herod; and at once the whole Church will feel herself struck in his person, and will not cease from offering her fervent prayers to God until he is delivered. Finally, on all occasions, Peter exercises in the infant Church that double prerogative of chief and centre with which Christ, before His Ascension, had invested him.

This mission has not ceased with Peter: it continues in his successors. Their See will be *par excellence*, and in the fullest sense of the word, the Apostolic See; and the term *Apostolicus* will be used until the end of time to designate the Pontiff seated on that throne. It is fitting, then, that the élite of the Christian Church who are striving to imitate the Apostolic life should ever be the most closely bound to the Apostolic See; so that neither increase of numbers, nor distance of place, nor the vicissitudes of time, should prevent their realizing that fruitful union of which so touching an example was offered by the faithful at Pentecost. We know that this union was, to our fathers, always an assured pledge of vitality and glory. Wherever the Benedictine monk turned his steps, he was considered as the born representative of Roman influence. Whether he is called Augustine in England, Willibrord in Frisia, Boniface in Germany, Adalbert in the Slav countries, it is always Rome who sends him, who blesses his beginning, seconds his efforts, and hallows his success. Having lent its assistance to the great liturgical work of Rome, and, side by side with the Roman faith, introduced civilization to the farthest boundaries of Europe, the monastic order will be called to a still higher mission. Identified for the time with the destinies of Rome, it will furnish, inspire, and support in every way those great Popes of the eleventh and twelfth centuries, the heroic defenders of the sanctity and independence of the Church.

After this epoch it begins, from various causes, to play a less important part. Nevertheless, it is an established and significant fact that the Popes have never ceased their efforts to protect and uphold it, and to attach it to themselves as the principal member to the head—*velut principalia capiti suo membra* (St Gregory VII, *Epist.* 69; Migne, 148, 420 B.) —to use the expression of our Gregory VII. Have we not ourselves had the happiness and consolation of witnessing the attachment of the last Pontiffs to our Order? Have they not often enough told us of the hopes which they built upon us? Let us respond to their confidence, ever remembering that the monk, to be faithful to his mission, must show himself "St Peter's man," the servant and the devoted son of the holy and Apostolic Church of Rome.

But it is impossible to embrace Rome by a loving faith without feeling all the pulsations of that Catholic life of which, providentially, she is the centre. There must, then, be nothing narrow in the soul of the monk. Whatever concerns the life of the Church, at any time and in all places, must find in him a faithful echo and a supernatural and practical sympathy. Whilst, with holy jealousy, he is careful to lose none of the treasures and venerable traditions stored up by the centuries in the bosom of the Church, he will not seek to isolate himself from any movement in Christian society inspired by the Holy Spirit. He suffers from each attack upon the Church, and would fain multiply himself, to avenge and defend her—at least, her needs are the chief burden of his prayers. He is wide in his petitions, for he remembers, like those glorious martyrs of Saragossa, whose acts we have all read, that he has to bear in his heart the whole Catholic Church from East to West.*

When there is a question of finding some direction for his natural activity, he, with the assistance of his Abbot, looks out over the vast extent of the Church of God, endeavouring to understand what are her present needs in such or such a country. Is not this what the men whom God has raised up in our time to revive and propagate the monastic order have done? Is it not this which, when once the traditions of Divine worship were re-established, led them to undertake in every country those works whose aim was to advance the salutary influence of the Church; whether by securing a Christian education to future generations, or by Apostolic missions for the preservation of the faith at home and abroad, or by literary and artistic works, which should continue among us the traditions of the glorious strivings of the past after the true and the beautiful; or, finally, by those organizations expressly formed for the solution of that great social problem in which the Church is ever ready to take a foremost part? We may sometimes feel overwhelmed by all these exterior works, joined to the burden, already sufficiently heavy, of the monastic life; and there is no denying that our life is more hurried and nervous than that of our fathers. But this is a necessity of the present day, when life moves more swiftly than of old. While the Church's unsleeping enemies never cease from their assaults, her sons must redouble their energy and zeal; nor must the monastic order remain in the rear, on pain of denying its past and imperilling its future. Doubtless its action will be somewhat solemn, commanding, and united, but none the less powerful, provided that each one

---

\* *In mente me habere necesse est ecclesiam catholicam ab oriente usque in occidentem diffusam* (*Acta SS. Fructuosi, Augurii, et Eulogii*, ap. Ruinart, *Acta Mart. sincera*).

brings to the movement of the whole that promptitude and self-abnegation which costs something to nature; but which, in the decisive moment, will secure success.

We are so much the better prepared for this call to arms because by our very profession we are made a kind of perpetual "reserve," pledged to keep the primitive spirit of Christianity in all its strength and integrity. This is the third characteristic of what we have called the Apostolic life; and we must say something about it, especially as it is the principal and indispensable condition of the life of a monk.

It may be said, without failing either in truth or reverence, that the Incarnate Word, who, as the Gospel tells us, vouchsafed to submit His mortal Body to the action of age and time, has not willed to exempt from it His mystical body, the Church. Though endowed with eternal youth, through the holy and radiant life which the Spirit continually renews within her, she has not passed through so many centuries without losing something of the freshness and energy of her early days. On her human side she seems at times to feel that weariness and exhaustion which her Divine Master deigned to experience when, wearied with the journey, He sat, at the sixth hour, beside the well of Samaria (John 4:6).

I am not speaking merely of those accidental forms which are to the Church what her ornaments are to a princess, and which she may change from age to age without showing any sign of decrepitude. Her temples may be in different styles; her liturgy may undergo modifications; her discipline, even, may be adapted to the necessities of modern times. This is not the important point. These are, rather, so many manifest proofs that she does not allow herself to be benumbed by that immovable rigidity which so early invaded the separated Churches. This is not the question. Of what, then, are we speaking? Of that ever-increasing decline of faith which, unless God intervene, threatens to lead the nations, formerly Christian, to the verge of that apostasy predicted by the Apostle (2 Thess. 2:3); of the lessening of the prestige of the Church, despoiled by revolutions of all which, humanly speaking, would insure her dignity and independence in the eyes of the people; of the comparative scarcity of men of great and profound learning, for which the increasing spread of education is far from supplying a remedy. What, then, is the question? It is, above all else, of the decrease, seen more clearly every day, of institutions and men dedicated to prayer, especially to the official, liturgical prayer of the Church; of the ease with which those who call themselves Christians dispense themselves from this great social duty, the public and visible sign of their communion with the rest of their brethren; finally, of that general forgetfulness of the holy rules of penance and mortification, whose absence is the strongest proof that the ideal of the Christian vocation is disappearing more and more, until at length it will be completely obliterated.

It is our duty, as monks, to counteract these manifold symptoms of deterioration. St Basil and the other Fathers of the monastic life taught this long ago; but we have a still better means of knowing it by glancing briefly through the Code of regular observance which St Benedict drew up for his monks. We shall see at once that most of the precepts sanctioned by him are only the remains of the discipline which formerly governed all Christian people. We have already seen this in speaking of work and of the distribution of necessaries; and we may affirm it with equal truth of the exceptional importance attached to liturgical prayer, with its different hours, going back in part to the very time of the Apostles, and to that rising in the night, so familiar to the primitive Christians. What is the abolition of individual property and the having all things in common but the reproduction of what went on in the bosom of the Church of Jerusalem? That strict repression of all crime, those public penances, those excommunications, if they do imply the ever-abiding weakness of the human element, can they, on the other hand, be considered as anything but a means of jealously keeping ourselves worthy of God and of His Christ? Those long hours consecrated to holy reading, the Gospel brought through prayer into the smallest events of daily life, those large-hearted traditions of hospitality and universal beneficence, those precepts relating to the maintenance of charity and peace, the close union of all the members with their hierarchical head—is not all this animated by the same breath which inspired the primitive documents of Christian literature, the letters of St Ignatius of Antioch, the *Pedagogue* and the *Stromata* of Clement of Alexandria, and the Acts of the most illustrious martyrs? Yes, there we shall find the true source of most of the points of our discipline, even to the abstinence from flesh of which the Apologists already boasted, and the Wednesday and Friday fasts observed since the first century of the Church.

Men often ask what can be the use and object of a Benedictine Abbey in our day. After what we have just seen, it is not difficult to reply that its use is more evident than ever; that its mission is to represent in the eyes of the people, concentrated as in a powerful focus, all the light and warmth, the strength and tenderness, the power and grandeur, the intensity of spiritual life within, as of beneficent and irresistible influence without, which are diffused throughout the great Church of God.

Every Christian, as he looks from afar on the lofty towers of these new Jerusalems, must feel a thrill of pride in belonging to the holy nation, to the Church; and from these should be able to picture to himself what this great Church would be if she everywhere enjoyed liberty of action, if the good seed were less mixed with the tares. In short, it should be impossible for anyone to cross the threshold of a Benedictine Abbey without sensibly realizing that Christian life of which so much is said and so little is known. We may maintain without paradox that, amidst the disappearance of so many ancient institutions, nothing at the present day can exercise an influence over society comparable to that of monastic Churches, built upon the broad foundations which befit them; an influence at once wide and deep, wholly supernatural from its beginning to its end; an influence, finally, which, as has been said, imitates so closely the action of that God, who is "Himself unmoved, all motion's source."

Once more, let us have a holy pride in God, in so noble a mission; and, without presumption as without hesitation, let us seek to realise it according to the measure of the gifts which God has meted to us. Let us work so as to deserve the praise which Holy Scripture gives to the first Christians, that at the last day our Lord may thus bear witness for us before the Angels and Saints: "These are men who have striven to the end fully to put into practice the teaching of My Apostles"—*And they were persevering in the doctrine of the apostles.*\*

---

\* *Erant perseverantes in doctrina apostolorum.*

## VI

## THE BREAKING OF BREAD

*Erant perseverantes… in communicatione fractionis panis.*
"And they continued steadfast in the breaking of the bread"
(Acts 2:42).

AFTER HAVING SAID in general terms that the primitive Christians conformed in all points to the teaching of the Apostles, the sacred writer mentions some of their ordinary practices. All these practices have manifestly a double object—to unite men to God and to unite men to one another. That was, in fact, the whole design of Jesus: *I in them, and thou in me; that they may be made perfect in one* *(John 17:23). It was the last word addressed to His Father in that grand sacerdotal prayer which He made for us before His death. We might, indeed, say that the unfailing criterion by which to judge of the value of a thing from the supernatural point of view consists chiefly in this: To examine if it helps or hinders the union of men with God, and, through God, that of men amongst themselves.

The passionate love of this unity has always been the clearest mark of the true Church and of the noblest spirits whom she has numbered in her fold. From the first they did not think it enough to maintain the essential unity of the faithful only by submission to one faith and to one visible authority. They also desired that this union of minds and hearts should be realised in the most perfect way, by a community of life which the fer-

* *Ego in eis, et tu in me: ut sint consummati in unum.*

vour and comparatively small number of the primitive Christians made possible and even easy. That was the ideal; and no truly great and holy person has ever appeared in the Church, even to the present day, who has not admired and envied it, and who has not tried to revive it, as far as lay in his power. It is so truly the nerve and vital strength of the Church that her enemies can never be mistaken about it. All the efforts of the pagan emperors had but one object—viz., to hinder the Christians from forming associations. The hatred of present-day sectaries never fails to begin its work by doing this whenever it can act freely—by forbidding every attempt at religious association, outlawing its members, even if it be necessary for this purpose to use violence as ridiculous as it is detestable.

However, let them do what they will; there will always be in the Church at least one kind of association which will last as long as the world. It is the Breaking of the Bread—the "synaxis," the Eucharistic sacrifice, that *dominicum* of which the martyrs accused of having taken part in it said: "We could not do without it. It must never be intermitted among us."\* In fact, still in our days the being present at the Sunday Mass and the receiving the Sacrament of the Lord at least once a year are the two indispensable conditions for being considered as a member of the Christian communion.

If the importance of the Eucharistic Sacrifice in the life of ordinary Christians is so great, it necessarily follows that far from

---

\* I celebrated the Lord's day with the brethren, because I am a Christian... it cannot be intermitted. Thus commands the law, thus teaches the law. We have most gloriously celebrated the assembly, because without the Eucharist, we cannot live.—*Dominicum cum fratribus celebravi, quia christiana sum. ... Non potest intermitti dominicum. Lex sic jubet, lex sic docet. Collectam gloriosissime celebravimus, quoniam sine dominico esse non possumus.*— Acta, s. Saturnini et soc., ap. Bolland. Tom., 2 Febr., p. 516 s.

losing anything of its dignity amongst us monks, it should be, so to speak, the luminous summit of the whole of our religious life. Therefore it is needful for us to get a correct and true idea of its grandeur, and this cannot be done better than by regarding it as our Fathers did, particularly St Augustine—that is to say, as the supreme sacrament of unity.*

It is from this eminently traditional point of view that we shall cast a rapid glance over its mysterious rites, reconstructing them as much as possible in their primitive amplitude, so as to comprehend more clearly their high symbolical meaning. It would be a sad thing if the study of the liturgy of the first Christian centuries—a study which has always been, and still is, held in honour by us—should serve only to satisfy the curiosity of archaeologists; we monks ought above everything to seek in it the living manifestations of a faith, young, ardent, and fresh from its source, so that we may in this point also fulfil our mission, which is, as we have seen, before all, conservative, though without exclusiveness of any kind.

This mark of unity appears first in the formation of the assembly; it is so, at any rate, in the great masses of the "Stations"—when the Christian population of a whole city collected round the Bishop and his clergy. And so, that this unity may be expressed clearly from the outset, a place of meeting is fixed upon, whence this

* Sermon CCXXVII: How you ought to love unity is commended to you in this bread (*Commendatur vobis in isto pane, quomodo unitatem amare debeatis*); Serm. CCXXIX: Behold what you have received. Therefore how you see what is done is one, thus be ye one (*Ecce quod accepistis. Quomodo ergo unum videtis esse quod factum est, sic unum estote vos*); Serm. LVII, n. 7: This virtue, which is here understood, is unity, that being brought together in His body, being made His members, we may be what we receive. *Virtus ipsa, quae ibi intellegitur, unitas est, ut redacti in corpus eius, effecti membra eius, simus quod accipimus*; in Joh., tract XXVI, n. 13: O sacrament of piety! O sacrament of unity! (*O sacramentum pietatis! O signum unitatis!*)

immense crowd will proceed together in majestic order to the principal basilica where the function is to be held. It is a similar motive which may have inspired our monastic custom of "stations." The faithful who are assisting must not for an instant show any kind of division, which could not be avoided if everyone straggled in, some early and some late. In the Canticle of Canticles the Church is compared to an army arranged in battle array: she has delighted in applying this figure to herself, and realizing it in those processions which mark the free and victorious character of her march through the ages, and whose impression upon the people is still unsurpassed and even unequalled.

At the moment when the prelate arrives at the altar he begins by saluting the Eucharist, reserved from a preceding Mass. By this sign of reverence he recognizes and sanctions what has been done in the former Mass (*synaxis*). He is not going to offer a new sacrifice, but to continue the same great and only sacrifice which, since it was first offered on Calvary, has filled all time and all space. His priesthood is the same as that of his predecessor, as that of his successors will be the same as his; for it is the same High Priest, established for ever, according to the Order of Melchisedek, who works yesterday, today, and for ever in the person of His ministers.

Then come the Lections given by one alone and listened to by all. Nothing is wanting, neither passages from the Law and the Prophets, nor the teaching of the Apostles, nor the heavenly doctrine of the Evangelists: for Jesus came not to destroy the Law and the Prophets, but to fulfil them. Thus all the monuments of the Divine revelation belong to us; the Church has preserved them all for us, the old and the new, from the *In principio* of Genesis to the "Amen" of the Apocalypse. What body of doctrine has ever offered such variety in a unity which goes on from the birthday of the world to the Marriage Feast of Eternity?

These Lections are interspersed with the chanting of the Psalms, whose rich modulations need all the skill of the solo singers of the Schola. But even from this the Christian people are not excluded—the last phrase is, at any rate, responded to by them. In places where it has been continued, the share taken by the whole assembly in the sacred chant which accompanies the celebration of the Mysteries is still a touching spectacle. We may say what we please about the inconveniences which from an artistic point of view result from any singing executed by a great crowd of people; but nothing will ever equal in the way of effect the impression of majestic and living unity which it produces; and since we regard it as part of our mission to work for the restoration of the venerable liturgical traditions, let us remember that there will always remain something to be desired, until we shall have given back to the people of God the active part which belongs to it—that grand chorus that no artificial combination can ever replace.

The Lections over, the solemn dismissal of all those who must not assist at the Sacrifice—properly so called—takes place: catechumens, penitents, or even simply those who do not communicate. It is unity accentuating and tightening its bonds; for all here must be in perfect concord. To allow anyone to be near the Holy Table who does not partake of it, is to expose the people assisting to the grievous scandal of a kind of schism. A vestige of this general communion of all the assistants has remained to our own day in the Mass of the Thursday in Holy Week. Formerly in our monasteries no great feast ever occurred without all, even the priests, receiving Communion from the hands of the Abbot. The custom has been modified, but the spirit remains the same. We may not assist at the Holy Mysteries without uniting ourselves to them, at least spiritually, with all the fervour of our souls.

The "Mass of the Faithful" begins with those prayers in the form of a Litany for all the needs of the Church, which we have retained in the Office of Good Friday. No intention is omitted in them: the Bishop and the whole hierarchy down to the monks and the widows, the civil powers, the sick, the poor, prisoners, travellers by land and water, the absent, those especially who are kept in mines or prisons on account of their faith; finally, heretics and schismatics, Jews and pagans, are in turn the object of a special prayer. It was while listening to this catalogue, in which nothing and no one is forgotten, that a great person who belonged to a separated Church was one day moved to tears, and repeated Solomon's words: *For she is the mother thereof!*\*

The very form in which the Church addresses her prayers to God is also in itself a sign of unity. It is a "Collect"—that is to say, a formula in which he who presides at the assembly gathers up the holy aspirations of each of its members, so as to offer them to God the Father through the Son, in the Holy Spirit.

But now we see the procession of sacred ministers advancing to the chancel-rail to receive the offerings of the faithful. Everyone knows that from the highest antiquity, even before the time of St Cyprian, these material offerings have been considered a striking symbol of the union which should reign among Christians. The wine, that drink which forms so complete a whole in the cup of Sacrifice is, nevertheless, made from many grapes mixed and pressed together. As to the bread, its symbolism is thus expressed in a ritual formula going back to the Apostolic age: "As the elements of this Bread scattered abroad upon the mountains, are gathered together in one, in like manner, O our Father, may Thy Church be gathered together from the ends of the Earth into Thy Kingdom." Even the few drops of

\* *Haec est enim mater ejus.*

water mixed with the wine have a part in the mystery of the union. The same Cyprian\* teaches us to see in them a figure of the share taken by the Christian people in the Sacrifice of the Incarnate Word, and such is indeed the meaning of the prayer which we still recite while mingling the water with the wine.

At length the Altar is approached. This Altar itself speaks to us of unity. According to the primitive spirit of the Church, not only is there but one Altar in the basilica, but, also, the sacrifice must not have been offered upon it before on that day, and it cannot be offered there again until the morrow: it was an almost absolute rule that the Eucharist could only be celebrated once a day at the same Altar. Our fathers considered it of importance, and the Orientals generally continue to conform to it. We may say that it is a trifle in itself: this is true. But this deep meaning attached to the smallest things relating to Divine worship sufficiently shows the eminently doctrinal character of ancient piety.

Anyone can see in the *Liturgical Year*, where it speaks of Corpus Christi, the primitive formula whence, in substance, our present Canon is derived. Nothing can compare with it for fulness; it is the most perfect act of thanksgiving that man can address to his Creator.

In it all the great benefits of God are, one by one, passed in review—the Creation, with all its marvels of nature and grace; then the Providential Economy of the Old Testament with its varied scenes and its multitude of figures. Ascending hence to the inaccessible focus of the Divinity, the celebrant humbly prays that the people present may join their voices with those

---

\* Ep. lxiii. 13: But when the water is mingled with the chalice of wine, the people are united with Christ, and the body of the believers are coupled with and joined to Him in whom they have believed—*Quando autem in calice vino aqua miscetur, Christo populus adunatur, et credentium plebs ei in quem credidit copulatur et iungitur.*

of the angelic choirs, and the imposing chant of the *Trisagion* realizes for a moment that sublime union of Heaven and Earth in the one great and true God.

Here the Act of Thanksgiving of the human race under the Judaical law might have terminated; but since then, God has given new gifts to Earth, and that which surpasses all the rest, His adorable Son, with all the other mysteries by which the redemption of the world has been accomplished. That is why the priest continues his Eucharist; he commemorates in turn the Incarnation of the Word, His mortal life and His Passion. At this moment, keeping close to the Gospel account, he recounts in detail the circumstances of the Last Supper, and declares that it is in order to continue what was then done, that the assembly offers to God this Eucharistic Bread and Wine. An invocation to the Holy Spirit, that He will realize on the oblation what He did in the Incarnation finishes the Mystery; and the Bishop immediately recommences the prayers for everything that concerns the life of the Church, for the living and the dead, the powers spiritual and temporal, and even for the fruits of the Earth.

Our Roman Canon has kept, in an abridged form, most of these features; some of them, perhaps, it even accentuates. Such is, in particular, that formula of the *Communicantes*, so little understood by people in general; it is, so to speak, the renewal of that salutation offered to the remains of the preceding Sacrifice, which opened the function. On the point of accomplishing the most solemn act of religion, the assembly feels the need of openly affirming its community in faith and charity with those who have gone before, and are now still united to them in Christ. Across time and space it takes by the hand the Apostles and Martyrs, all those who profess the same orthodox Faith, so as to join them in a manner with the act which it is going to renew after them and with them. Such was formerly the high signification of that reading of the sacred dyptichs, that to erase a name from them was equivalent to the most formal sentence of excommunication which could be pronounced in the Church. The *Supplices te rogamus*, which follows the consecration, is no less full of mystery. Instead of beseeching, according to the Eastern use, the descent of the Spirit on the oblation, the Church asks, on the contrary, that it may be carried by the hand of the Angel of the Lord to the altar on high, in the presence of the Divine Majesty; so that the earthly Sacrifice may form but one with that of Heaven, and produce in our souls the same effects of grace.

At the conclusion of the Canon it was formerly the custom to bless certain first-fruits intended for the food of the faithful. It is still at this period of the Mass, before the *Pater*, that on Holy Thursday the blessing of the Holy Oils takes place—a new manner of expressing the close connection of every benediction, even temporal, with the supreme one which changes the Eucharistic Species into the Body and Blood of the God-Man.

But it is above all in the Communion rites that the Church of Rome has sought to express in the clearest way ecclesiastical unity. It is begun by the Kiss of Peace, in which all who communicate must take part. In our monasteries, on days when the priests themselves communicated at the High Mass, this rite was performed in a more complete and striking manner than at present. The Abbot first gave the kiss to the Prior, then the oldest monk received it from both the Abbot and the Prior, as afterwards the monks in succession in order of profession; so that each one embraced not only his neighbour, but the whole community ranged around the Altar. This would seem to us, at the present day, too long and too complicated; but it would be a touching pledge of perfect unanimity, at the moment when all are going to partake of the Victim offered on the Altar; and how would not every shadow of dissension disappear before such a demonstration!

But now the celebrant has put into the chalice the particle of the consecrated Host which was brought to him at the commencement of the Mass, so that he may unite It with his own Sacrifice. He then divides his own Host, and mingles a fragment of It in the same way with the Precious Blood. From the remainder he will also break off a portion to put It with the particles destined for the communion of the clergy and people; in the same manner the Archdeacon will pour a few drops out of the chalice from which the celebrant has first drunk, into the larger one intended for the faithful. St Paul's idea must be clearly explained: Though there are many cups and many patens containing Hosts, there is but one Food, but one spiritual Drink, transmitted to all the Christian people, by but one and the same hierarchical head— *We who all partake of one bread*\*(1 Cor. 10. 17).

This sacred sign of communion will soon cross the narrow limits of the temple where the assembly is held. A portion of the Bread consecrated at the Episcopal Mass will be sent to every parish priest, and no one within the circuit of the city may celebrate the mystery of the Eucharist without having first received that *fermentum* destined to be united with his own consecration, as a forceful expression of the union of the whole Church with its shepherd. Thus there is, always and everywhere, the same Sacrifice, always and everywhere the same faith, always and everywhere the same charity "in the bond of peace."

Perhaps these details, many of which have fallen entirely into disuse, while others are rarely observed, may have wea-

\* *Omnes qui de uno pane participamus.*

ried the reader. But nothing is more effectual for bringing to our minds and hearts the full understanding of all that there is for us monks in that venerable Sacrifice in which we daily take part. Doubtless, simple faith may be sufficiently built up upon the words of the sacred books relating to the institution of this mystery; but God has willed that we should not be satisfied with that. The words and ceremonies which accompany the celebration of the Eucharist ought to be looked upon by us as stamped with a deep meaning: Jesus and His Apostles regulated a certain number of them; the others are the purest expression of what was thought and felt by our fathers in the Faith, on the subject of this great legacy of the Saviour. Those which we have retained have no other source; if we wish to perform them with an enlightened conscience, with a comprehension as complete as possible of the smallest details, nothing will help us so well as going back to this source; carefully and lovingly studying everything that touches the origin of Catholic worship, and especially the most sublime act of this worship—the Sacrifice of the Altar. It is one of the duties of the novitiate, but it can only begin there; a good monk will keep all his life the same zeal for increasing, from this point of view, his treasure of spiritual knowledge. And, in order to practise it, it is an excellent thing, as we have sometimes been told, to look over again from time to time, especially during the annual exercises, the text itself of the rubrics and the Canon, in order to prevent the inevitable dangers of routine and inadvertence in the celebration of so sublime a Sacrifice.

As to the manner of assisting at Holy Mass, it can hardly be that we should not prefer what is in common, and what best expresses unity, to even the sweetest practices of private devotion. I know of a monastery where it was necessary one day to call to order some very good brothers, who deserted the

Communion Mass celebrated at the High Altar on Sunday after Lauds, to go and assist furtively at a private Mass in some remote corner of the Church. To act thus, without a serious and reasonable motive, simply to satisfy the desire for recollection, certainly came from an insufficient comprehension of the nature and true bearing of the holy Sacrifice. In the same way with us in Lent, and on fast days, when we have several conventual Masses, it is always a beautiful thing to see a certain number of monks representing the community in a befitting manner, thus replacing, or at least deferring for a time, some other practice of devotion.

The same principle will guide us in the choice of a method of assisting at the Divine Liturgy. There are all kinds of ways, composed for the most part by persons noted for their holiness, but most of which have this fault, that they separate the soul more or less from what is going on at the Altar. After having tried them all, one after another, one returns instinctively to the ancient and simple method of following what is done with the eye, what is said and sung with the ear, and with the heart what is beneath all this—the vital Mystery of Christianity, that Breaking of Bread which is, here below, our greatest means of union, until we arrive at that more perfect union in the bosom of eternal joys which we ask of God in one of the prayers after the Communion—*That what we do in this life we may follow in the joys of eternity*\* (Post-Communion of the Wednesday in Whitsuntide).

---

\* *Ut quod temporaliter gerimus, aeternis gaudiis consequamur.*

# VII
# LITURGICAL PRAYER

*Erant perseverantes in orationibus*
"And they were persevering in prayers" (Acts 2:42).

THE BREAKING OF the Bread was the especial duty of Christ's disciples; but they were no less faithful to the great duty of prayer, the ancient obligation, the normal position of the creature who desires to keep himself in his proper place towards his Creator. That is why the author of the Acts, after those words *They were persevering in the communication of the breaking of bread,*\* adds immediately, *and in prayers.*† They also persevered in prayer.

It may be asked of what kind of prayer St Luke speaks in this passage: of the liturgical prayer—that is, of the Office—or of private prayer, left to each one's devotion. We see from the course of the account that the Apostles and their converts devoted themselves to both these kinds of prayer. Like all pious Israelites, they went regularly to the Temple, there to give praise to God; besides assisting daily at the morning and evening sacrifice, they observed faithfully the practice of going to the Court of the Temple for the public prayer of the third, sixth, and ninth hour. We also see them practising private prayer on many occasions. Since we also have both these kinds of prayer, and as both play a most important part in our monastic life, it will not be too much to dedicate a special conference to each of

\* *Erant perseverantes in communicatione fractionis panis.*
† *Et orationibus.*

them. Let us begin with the great liturgical prayer. It seems that the monk should always be, like the youngest of Job's friends, "full of words," when the subject is one so dear to his heart; and yet it is a fact that nothing is more difficult than to speak worthily of the Divine Office; I mean, to avoid exaggeration and to find the true reason for the place which it occupies in our life. St Benedict puts in the foremost rank among the conditions that every postulant must fulfil, zeal for the work of God. And as to professed monks, he will not allow them to put anything before it. It is that which obliges us to assign to the Office its exceptional place in the obligations of our condition. Does it follow that we must be satisfied, especially at the present time, with the old formula, that monks are *established for the choir*,* and believe that our whole spiritual activity should be absorbed by psalmody, the chanting of antiphons, responses, and hymns? Is it even correct to present the chanting of the Office as the specially characteristic side of the Benedictine vocation?

This has been said, and often repeated, particularly since the sixteenth century. Suarez taught it in his voluminous theological works; Dom Guéranger, the restorer of monastic life in France, has made this principle the foundation of his reform. In spite of all the respect due to such authorities, the formula may conceal a misunderstanding which should be explained before going farther.

In the first place, we should vainly seek in the Rule for a trace of the assertion that the Divine Office is the object of the monastic life. It is true that the Canonical hours are there carefully regulated; it is also true that St Benedict enjoins that everything must be interrupted in order to be present when the time for them comes; but the rest of the day not consecrated to the Divine Office he divides equally between study

* *Propter chorum fundati.*

and work, and it is nowhere said that this study and this work must have direct reference to "the work of God," save for a few moments for those who still need instruction in the singing of the Psalms, or have to prepare themselves for some office of the Choir. In short, Canonical prayer is, without doubt, the noblest of the elements of the Benedictine life, because it refers directly to God; but, after all, it leaves room for many kinds of activity, without being the necessary and indispensable end of all the rest. Its chosen place among all the exercises of the monk simply corresponds with that which it held in the regard and in the daily life of the primitive Christians. This, then, is another consequence of the principle laid down before, that the vocation of the monk is to carry on to the end of time the spirit and traditions of the Church of the first centuries.

There is no question as to whether the performance of liturgical functions may become the particular aim of a religious body; that is not the point in dispute; but, as a matter of fact, that is by no means a special prerogative of our Order. If any Order has the right to boast of this it is the Canons Regular, rather than ourselves. That one of the latest offshoots of the Benedictine tree has made liturgical life its almost exclusive ideal is a kind of local phenomenon, which has had its providential *raison d'être*. Just as we have seen some Congregations of our Order devote themselves specially either to the cultivation of the land, the service of the poor and of pilgrims, or to great and learned literary works, so the mission of the French Congregation has been that assigned to it by its Brief of Erection—namely, to restore the imperilled traditions of liturgical unity, and thereby to prepare that movement of return to Rome which is the great fact of the ecclesiastical history of the nineteenth century. This, again, was the ordering of Providence. Certainly the task is far from being completed, and there is still much to be done in different countries to bring it to a good end; but we are not concerned here with particular circumstances; we want to get a clear idea of our vocation, and of the place which different elements occupy in it.

Now, the singing of the Divine Office, though it ought to hold the foremost place in our esteem, as in that of the first Christians, was never—at least, until modern times—considered as the mark of our vocation. Until the sixteenth century no order ever sprang up in the Church which did not retain the Choir Office, making it, at least in theory, its first duty. Thus, the Friars Preachers inscribed on the first page of their *Declarations* the *solemn recitation of the divine office*,* and history shows us their holy founder going continually from side to side of the choir during Matins, to excite the religious to sing "loudly and devoutly"—*ut alte et devote cantarent*. Almost all the other Orders can show like instances, drawn either from their Constitutions or from the lives of their Saints.

Nevertheless, the nearer we come to modern times, the less we find the liturgical life understood and appreciated. We can understand this, for each of the institutions founded after the thirteenth century proposed to itself a definite end, and corresponding to some actual need of the Church. Thenceforward everything else was valued only so far as it contributed to the realisation of that end.

The solemn celebration of the Divine Office became simply a means, as any other; and soon the highest intellects, led by St Thomas, regarded the Divine praises in this light, declaring that they were inferior in nobility and efficacy to the ministry of preaching—*To arouse men to devotion by teaching and preaching is a more excellent way than by singing.*†

---

\* *Sollemnis officii divini recitatio.*
† *Nobilior modus est provocandi homines ad devotionem per doctrinam et praedicationem quam per cantum* (*Summa Theolog.*, 2. 2, q. 91, a. 2, ad 3).

In the same passage of his *Summa* the Master of the schools considers the sacred chant only as a useful means of exciting devotion in the weak. We must confess that we are very far, and shall soon be still farther, from our predecessors' idea of the excellence of the Divine Office. The older the world grows, the more utilitarian it becomes; life is everywhere fuller; the enemies of the Church multiply and grow bolder day by day, thus giving more work to her defenders, who are compelled to work at higher pressure. "What is the use of continuing those choir exercises which hitherto have taken up so much time, and whose practical utility is more and more disputed?" And so it is that we have seen for the first time a regular army, which ever since its formation has dispensed itself from this obligation, which until then had been considered essential to all Religious Orders.

Doubtless, God had His own designs in allowing the spirit of the age to follow its natural bent, and the Church adapted herself as ever to her new surroundings. But, none the less, this has resulted in a kind of isolation for our Order, and because it has remained strongly attached to liturgical traditions, it will soon be considered as being no longer abreast of the times. The world has come to regard as a special vocation that which for thirteen hundred years was the patrimony of Christian society. Perhaps, on its own part, the Order has too easily resigned itself to the diminished role assigned to it. Entrenched in its Abbeys, which have become too large, it takes, as a rule, too little interest in the exterior life of the Church. The consequence is that, in proportion to its ever decreasing influence, its recruits have declined in number and value.

How is this fact to be explained?

It is clear, in the first place, that this paltry way of considering liturgical life only from a practical and utilitarian point of view—that is, simply in its relation to the edification of the

Christian people, was by no means that of our fathers. Very frequently access to monastic churches was expressly forbidden to the faithful; sometimes the assistance of outsiders was so insignificant that there could be no proportion between the pomp displayed in the choir and the number of strangers admitted to witness it. Therefore, if the monks did devote so much of their time, both by day and night, to the Divine praises, it was for themselves alone, a matter between themselves and God. It was, with them, the natural efflorescence of a fresh and overflowing love of God, joined to that other love of brethren living in common—the two foundations of monastic society, as, in its beginning, of Christian society also.

Saint Augustine delighted to repeat those beautiful words, *Cantare amantis est*—to sing is the work of a lover. This is most true. Speech is sufficient for the expression of a man's ordinary thoughts; but let a stronger or sweeter emotion take possession of his heart, and as if by instinct he will lift up his voice; the monotone of habitual speech no longer satisfies him, and he will sing; with the Psalmist he will ask that his mouth may be filled with songs. *May my mouth be filled with praise, that I may sing.*\* Song, then, especially sacred song, is above all a manifestation of love. But this manifestation is not for everyone; it supposes a certain youthful ardour, which is not ashamed to manifest itself in all its naivete. Who sing more or better than children and young people? But as man grows older disillusions and disenchantment multiply, enthusiasm cools, and at last vanishes altogether; a half sceptical smile curls the lips which once sang of love; and if some notes should still come from them they are for the most part only echoes of sorrow.

Here, as elsewhere, the life of a people follows the same course as that of the individual. Why is it that in the begin-

\* *Repleatur os meum laude, ut possim cantare.*

ning of all literature we invariably find hymns, or sacred odes, but because it is the natural manifestation of the first love of a youthful nation? But as we trace the literary history of any people, we see this enthusiasm for religious poetry less and less cultivated, as men's minds take a more and more positive direction, until at last hardly any works are held in estimation except studies in philology, criticism, or mathematics. When a nation has become old, its sacred inspiration can never flourish again unless its youth be renewed by some great convulsion followed by a new infusion of moral blood, such as that which took place in the first half of the nineteenth century.

What we have just said of song applies to every manifestation of feeling. Look at any nation which has not become cold by contact with our civilization, and see what a demonstrative character everything assumes, how frankly and candidly men show what they think and feel. Let us recall those descriptions of ancient hospitality of which we read in the most beautiful pages of history, both sacred and profane, that innocent freedom in the expression of mutual affection. All is simple, true, and unconstrained, and is the spirit and even the letter of our Rule. We need only read again the chapter *Of the reception of guests*\* with its directions concerning the washing of the hands and feet of the guests by the Abbot and the whole community, and the kiss of peace, given after all have prayed together. Our *Opus Dei*† was, in its origin, only one of those expressive manifestations which denote a people still young and capable of loving. We may be very sure that it would not have been instituted in our day. And why? Because society has grown old, and more and more formal and prudish in the display of even its most praiseworthy interior feelings, above all, religious

---

\* *De hospitibus suscipiendis.*
† *Work of God.*

feelings. Why do our profound reverences seem so strange to some people, even priests? Why do we see the almost universal suppression of that harmless mark of hospitality, the washing of the hands of the guests by the Abbot, still, however, practised here and there, even in these latter days? Why does the kiss of peace, formerly so common in the Christian life, tend more and more to be replaced by that frigid handshake which seems made on purpose to keep a man at a respectful distance? Why has this same kiss, prescribed by liturgical rules for the most solemn moment of the Holy Sacrifice, become almost everywhere only a formal and meaningless salutation?

Doubtless, it would be difficult, if not impossible, entirely to escape being influenced by our effete society; but at least we shall not degenerate, so long as we are faithful to the precept which St Benedict has left us, lovingly to fulfil the noble work of the praises of God. We may sacrifice certain details; but so long as we feel in our hearts that same zeal for the Work of God that we had on coming to the monastery, so long as we are not contented to prefer a system of spirituality which economizes time, strength, and I know not what beside, let us take comfort, for if to this we join sincere obedience, we are true monks. Here, then, is the explanation of the problem which we set ourselves at the beginning. We now understand why the love of the Divine Office is the indispensable sign of all monastic vocation, above all in our own day. It is not so much the Office in itself that signifies, but rather the disposition which it implies in the soul of him who is called to fulfil it. It requires, in fact, a soul capable not only of loving God, and in Him all that is lovable, great, beautiful, and noble; but more than this—rich enough in youth and enthusiasm to bear with courage the real burden of the sacred psalmody and not to be daunted by a life in which the chant and the outward signs of interior devotion will to the end occupy so important a place: a soul sufficiently imbued with the charity and Catholic spirit of earlier times, to fear isolation even in its relations with God, and to understand that Jesus is never nearer to it than when its voice is joined to those of its brothers, gathered together in His name. Obedience is required of us as religious, love of the Office is indispensable to us as monks; the first is the condition necessary for all community life, the second is the distinguishing mark of the disciple of St Benedict. Everything has been said when once the postulant has been able to answer "Yes" to the three questions: *Whether he is zealous for the Work of God, for obedience and for humiliations.*\* Now, the third point being only the perfecting of the second, we shall be right to simplify it still further by saying that these two things—love of the Divine Office and Obedience—are sufficient.

If we have thoroughly understood the foregoing reflections on the significance of liturgical life amongst us, and the atmosphere which it necessarily implies, many things will at the same time have been made clear. In the first place, the comparative rarity of Benedictine vocations. We must not deceive ourselves: we are altogether both too old and too young for the speedy establishment between us and modern society of those friendly relations which usually suppose equality of age. Too old, because many details of our life, especially our liturgical life, are stamped with that impress of past ages of which the present generation naturally sees only the archaic character without suspecting the life-giving savour: too young, because too unreserved in the outward tokens of our fear of God, our love, and respect for holy things, for authority, and for everything exalted and beautified by faith. But this is no reason for discouragement, still less for giving up. The restoration of monasticism

\* *Si sollicitus sit ad opus Dei, ad obedientiam, ad opprobria.*

coincides with an epoch of ferment and social reform. It is not without a merciful design of Providence that we have not seen a Benedictine Abbey in our country for nearly a century. Had we lived on after the Revolution, we might have passed as the worn-out remnant of an old institution whose days are none the less numbered because by chance it has escaped the storm. On the contrary, appearing today after so long an interval, we find ourselves with youth renewed, transplanted, as it were, to a virgin soil (the learned alone can tell our precise age): and although this youth springs in great part from the things which we have saved out of the past, all the vigour and resource for the future that there is in modern surroundings sympathises naturally with us.

How many prejudices have already been overcome, what an unhoped-for turning has there been towards all the great and beautiful things which we have kept alive amongst us—liturgical music, medieval Christian art, patient research in the vast field of ecclesiastical tradition! The rest will come in its own time; and that hour we can hasten by multiplying around us the tokens of that Christian life, ever ancient and ever new, which it is our mission to fulfil until the end of time. This, after the grace of God, will be the principal source of our vocations. Let us act towards society without either weakness or rigidity, neither condemning what it lawfully loves, nor giving up that which we ourselves are bound to prefer before everything; and the world will soon feel that we are not strangers, and will give us its sons to become our brothers.

Various important conclusions, relating to the performance of the Divine Office, result from this. There is one point which calls for special attention, and that is the Chant. In our time, the Benedictines have had the glory of taking the lead in restoring and propagating true Gregorian Chant. But since then much ground has been gained; to the tentative and individual efforts of the first days has succeeded a veritable science of chant, founded on well-established principles, at least in broad outline, and involving in its execution practical consequences which we must take into account, if we would not run the risk of being left in the rear. We have already rejoiced to see seculars throwing themselves into the movement; it would be a pity to let ourselves be passed by them, almost at the outset! Let each do his own part—some by keeping themselves well-informed as to the theory, others by learning the correct rendering of the melodies from those who possess the secret. The matter is of extreme importance, not merely from the artistic point of view—which here is only secondary—but, above all, for the full and entire preservation of the monastic spirit. If ever, which God forbid, the liturgical chant should come to be neglected among us—if the long hours passed in Choir should be changed, little by little, into an exercise purely material and unaesthetic—that moment would give the deathblow to enthusiasm for Divine worship—that enthusiasm without which, as we have said, there can be no true monks. Certainly it is a matter which requires effort; but let us remember the words of St Augustine: *To sing is the work of a lover.*\* And what is there that is impossible or even difficult to love?

---

\* *Cantare amantis est.*

# VIII
# MONASTIC SPIRITUALITY

We will again consider the text: "They were persevering in prayer."

IT WOULD BE a mistake to suppose that the monk could be content in the matter of prayer, with the *official* prayer, that is, the Divine Office. Psalmody is before all things an action, the *Opus Dei*, but it is an action which presupposes contemplation, either as a preparation or a result. Under the first aspect psalmody is the highest expression of the soul's admiration for that God, to approach Whom is continually to renew its youth; considered under the second, it is itself a very powerful means of speeding the soul's flight towards the blessed state of contemplation. Our fathers well understood that these two kinds of prayer were inseparable from one another, and therefore they directed that at the end of each psalm and before each collect of the Office there should be intervals of silence, during which, prostrate before God, each one might pour out the affections which the holy psalmody had suggested, or ponder those intentions which the president of the assembly should afterwards offer to God in the name of all the assistants. This is what Saint Benedict calls the *reverentia orationis—reverence in prayer*. The thing has been abolished, the principle remains: the monk will gather but little fruit from his assistance at the Divine Office if he do not join to it these *orationes peculiares*, those pious exercises which, taken all together, form the tribute due from every soul called to that closer intercourse with God which we generally call the "spiritual life."

Monastic spirituality, then, is the subject which naturally presents itself to us, after treating of liturgical prayer.

Here, for the moment, we find ourselves on strange ground. For three hundred years, in all parts of the Church, the Holy Spirit has directed new currents of devotion in accordance with the ordinary state of souls living in the world. Although living under totally different conditions, the monk neither can nor ought to remain altogether outside these movements. Only there is a proper limit to be observed, and that is not always easy. We are enthusiastic over new methods, more practical, subtler, and more refined; we surrender without regret that which hitherto has been the basis of the spiritual life in our cloisters, to take up eagerly with new principles, new books, new devotional recipes. In short, things have come to such a pass that many Benedictines have ended by letting themselves be taken in tow by modern institutions, whose origin and tendencies are quite unlike their own, thus losing sight of their past, and hindering the normal and natural development of their own spirituality by the indiscreet introduction of elements, good in themselves, but designed for needs quite other than theirs.

The misfortune is that it is not so easy to regain possession of our old principles of spirituality, as to re-establish those of discipline adapted to the true character of our constitution. As to these last, the ground is clear: there is nothing to prevent us from following the pure inspirations of tradition and of the Holy Rule; in fact, we have only too much choice, so abundant are the sources from which we may draw. But it is quite otherwise when we come to the details of the spiritual life. On all sides there is an endless variety of methods and practices to which for the most part we have long been accustomed; a perfect swarm of little books, good and substantial, which once we prized highly. But we shall not have been long in the monastery before we perceive that there is something forced and artificial in all this—something which does not entirely square with the breadth and simplicity of our life. On the other hand, we shall find little or nothing which seems to us capable of taking the place of this little armoury of devotion. These little books which seem quite indispensable to most people nowadays were hardly dreamt of by our forefathers; we shall not find amongst us, until we come to the fifteenth century, anything which anticipates the Exercises of Saint Ignatius, and then only in manuscript, or rare books, and in a style too laboured to suit our modern taste. So that when the novice comes to the monastery he finds for his code of spirituality only a Rule, whose spiritual treasures he is as yet unable to suspect, together with some unusual practices which have escaped the shipwreck of our traditions, such as visits to the altars and other like things.

Here there is a real objection which it is important to obviate, by trying to get a clear idea of monastic spirituality and its relation to modern spirituality.

We have said more than once that the life of society becomes daily busier, more restless and nervous; that that *otium sanctum*, that holy leisure in which the greater part of the lives consecrated to God were once passed, has become a rare thing on the earth. Nevertheless, the soul must have its assured means of subsistence. What, then, must be done? We have all seen those little tabloids containing sufficient condensed nourishment to allow of our taking long and fatiguing journeys without spending time and money on regular meals. This idea in its application to the life of the soul has been worked out in later times by the leaders of the ascetic movement. Glance over the different methods of devotion most in vogue—for example, that of Saint Sulpice, which is perhaps the most perfect of all—study them, analyze them, dissect them. You will find that this prodigious result has been reached—the bringing into the compass of an exercise intended to occupy half, or at most three-quarters, of an hour, all the sentiments and movements of the soul possible to any of the fathers of the desert or to the holy men of all times put together. Many of the exercises in use in seminaries and modern communities were introduced in view of this necessity. Three or four years at most are consecrated to the formation of the clerical students; in this short time we are obliged to instil into them as strong a dose as possible of spirituality; or, to use another simile, commonplace, but permissible, they have to be "forced," like plants.

Afterwards, absorbed in the thousand cares of daily ministry, hardly finding time to say their Office, on what can their souls live without that poor half-hour of meditation, intended for the renewal of their strength morning by morning?

It is evident that the monk's case is altogether different. From his entrance into the Abbey until he leaves it by death, his life is mostly passed in that relative leisure which is for him, on the warrant of our Lord Himself, the good part, Mary's part. Thenceforward, all that more or less artificial system of modern asceticism will not suffice him. He needs something more simple and natural, less dainty, but not less strengthening. The monk need not make plans; he is not like most men, absorbed by cares for the future. Like those birds of the air of which Jesus speaks in the Sermon on the Mount, the monk has no barns to fill; even for the nourishment of his soul his daily bread is sufficient, and he confidently awaits his Heavenly Father's bounty. He knows that at any moment he can find the food necessary for his soul in the ever-verdant pastures of Holy Scripture, or in the rich harvest-fields of the writings of the

Fathers and Doctors of the Church. Accustomed to abandon his life to the sweet providence of God, he has no reason for being more anxious on one day than another; he need not even store up more of the Heavenly manna on the eve of the Sabbath than during the rest of the week: his Sabbath, his only true rest, is Heaven. The Bridegroom never visits him without saying to him as to the Spouse in the Canticles: "Open to Me, My beloved, for My head is filled with dew, and My locks with the drops of the night" (Cant. 5:2). This is an exact image of the monk's life of grace. Upon others, more exposed to the drought of the world, to the burden and heat of the day, and the fatigue of a fierce conflict, grace falls at times; fast and abundantly it is true, but like the quickly passing thunder-rain, or the rush of the torrent. For us grace is a dew—that morning and evening dew so often promised in Scripture, which sinks gently into the soil, opens the buds in their due season, and gives refreshment and fruitfulness to the fields.

Perhaps some may say: This is all very well, but, after all, what is our exact position with regard to modern spirituality? Must we refuse to touch any of its productions? Must we contemn its methods, its tendencies, all its books, little and great?

God forbid! The counsel of the Apostle will always hold good for reasonable men—*But prove all things; hold fast that which is good*\* (1 Thess. 5:21). No, we must in nowise be understood as rejecting wholesale the productions of modern asceticism; firstly, because all this movement is linked with the action of the Holy Ghost, the life of the Church, the influence of holy persons of these later days—and it would be rashness in a Catholic, whoever he might be, to whatever Order he might belong, completely to separate himself from these manifestations of the Christian spirit of our time. Finally because, even

\* *Omnia probate, quod bonum est tenete.*

outside the monastic movement, many phenomena of sanctity, many movements of asceticism, have arisen in the Church, worthily carrying on the traditions of former ages, of which we may make use without fear of in any way compromising our own life.

What true monk may not lawfully take pleasure in St Francis de Sales' treatise *On the Love of God*, in the writings of St Teresa; or even more recent authors, such as Father Faber or Mgr. Gay?

A last reason which must be taken into account is, that although the contemplation of the things of God must always, in principle at least, be the supreme end of our vocation, the monastic life has been obliged to adapt itself in more than one point to the requirements of our age. Without following it in its absorbing activity, which hardly leaves the soul time to breathe, we cannot deny that certain monastic communities, or at least certain members of those communities, sometimes risk the loss of the necessary leisure to respond to the Psalmist's invitation: *Be still and see*\* (Ps. 45:11). It was wise, therefore, to extend to all, in a certain measure, the benefits of those modern expedients intended to assure to each man of goodwill at least the minimum of time necessary for attending to God and the things of his soul.

Hence those wise directions in most of our monastic Constitutions touching the daily half-hour's meditation, the examination of conscience after Compline, and the exercises of the annual retreat. But must we stop short at this? Clearly not; above all if the grace of God and the counsel of the Abbot have made us realise more perfectly the ideal of the monastic life from this point of view.

It may, perhaps, be asked, in what this ideal consists. In one word: in raising gently, very gently, the level of all the powers of the soul, enlarging peacefully and regularly all the avenues

\* *Vacate et videte.*

through which God comes to it, so that it may be filled with all the fulness of Him, Who, to use St Augustine's words, is the Food of the strong: *I am the food of the full-grown; grow, and thou shalt feed on Me*\* (*Confessions*, Lib. VII., chap. 10). To arrive at this, we must before all have an exact idea of the contemplative life, as it was understood in our Order and in the Church, up to the thirteenth century, and of the manner in which various practices of modern piety, such as spiritual reading, meditation, prayer, and contemplation, properly so called, have been grafted upon it.

We will begin by speaking of the difference. What we have already said will have sufficed to show it; it is chiefly that what was formerly united in one simple and natural whole is now divided systematically into so many acts or distinct states, each having its work clearly specified, its fixed term—except the last—contemplation—which is considered only the exceptional privilege of certain souls in a higher state of grace. The meditation must be made at such an hour in the morning, for so long a time: spiritual reading in the evening at a certain hour; prayer at given moments during the day; and so of the rest. This was not the system of our holy Father, nor that which was in use for nearly a thousand years after his time. There were no arbitrary separations, no special hours assigned to each of the phenomena of the interior life. Doubtless all these are there; but each one springs up spontaneously in its own hour, or, rather, in the hour of the Holy Spirit, who works in souls when He pleases, and as long as He pleases. St Benedict, in each of his rules regarding prayer, desires before all to respect this sovereign liberty of the Holy Spirit: *Unless it chance to be prolonged by the impulse and inspiration of divine grace*† (Rule, ch. 20). That

---

\* *Cibus sum grandium; cresce et manducabis me.*
† *Nisi forte ex affectu inspirationis divinae gratiae protendatur.*

*any brother who may wish to pray privately be not hindered... if anyone wish to pray secretly, let him just go in and pray*\* (ch. 52).

In the Rule there is but one thing having a fixed time assigned to it, and that is the *lectio divina*—the reading of the things of God. The reason is clear: reading is the common treasury, the habitual place of refuge for the soul, the starting-point in its flight towards God. How is this? St Thomas explains it admirably in his *Summa* (2. 2, q. 180, a. 3, *ad.* 4), but perhaps Guigo the Carthusian explains it still better in his treatise, *De modo orandi* (under the title of *Scala paradisi* in the appendix of volume vi of St Augustine; and of *Scala claustralium* among the small works wrongly attributed to St Bernard). Man does not in one moment arrive at the supreme act of the spiritual life, which is the contemplation of truth. Before he undertakes to traffic with God, he must borrow the material from Him.

Sometimes God takes it on Himself to make the advances; in His merciful condescension He suddenly and without any intermediary fills a soul, hitherto ignorant, with the overflowing communications of His Divine wisdom. But such cases are comparatively rare, and it would be folly to count upon them in practice. To make progress in the spiritual life it is not enough, generally speaking, either to show ourselves faithful in action, or even to address ourselves directly to God in prayer; we must, also, have recourse to the human means placed at our disposal for making the truth sink into our souls. Now, the truth may be received in the first place through the ear, by hearing it explained by the living voice of those appointed to instruct us; and this is one of the things which St Benedict

---

\* *Frater, qui forte sibi peculiariter vult orare, non impediatur.... Si alter vult sibi forte secretius orare, simpliciter intret et oret.*

allows us to hope for from our Abbot, for he wishes him to be, before all else, a man of doctrine (Rule, ch. 64).

But, again, it is only at comparatively rare intervals that we hear the human word, and, moreover, the same food may not be suitable for all at the same moment. It is, then, from reading that we commonly draw the first principles necessary for our advancement. And so the Holy Rule assigns a very considerable part of the day to this reading—never less than from two hours in the summer to five in the winter, and even more in Lent. As to the rest, there could not be a greater freedom than St Benedict leaves us in the choice of books for this reading—not only every page of Holy Scripture, properly so called, but any writing whatsoever of the Fathers of the Church—is, according to him, a sure rule of human life, and should serve to bring us straight to our Creator—*For what page or what utterance of the divinely inspired books of the Old and the New Testament is not a most unerring rule of human life? Or what book of the holy Catholic Fathers is not manifestly devoted to teaching us the straight road to our Creator?*\*(Rule, ch. 73).

We cannot sufficiently admire the breadth of such a doctrine. At the present day we have become so fastidious and so hard to please that we have ended by seriously curtailing the number of books profitable for our souls.

Whatever is put into our hands, no matter whether it be some masterpiece of the greatest doctors, St Augustine, St Gregory, or any other, our first impulse is to be ill-humoured and contemptuous. To our idea anything profitable to the

---

\* *Quae enim pagina, aut quis sermo divinae auctoritatis veteris ac novi Testamenti non est rectissima norma vitae humanae? Aut quis liber sanctorum catholicorum Patrum hoc non resonat, ut recto cursu perveniamus ad creatorem nostrum?*

soul in these books is drowned by a sea of mystical reflections which only hinder our impatient and over-nice devotion. We are tempted to prefer some little book where we shall find the same spiritual marrow, but without either flesh or bones. Such is not the taste of St Benedict, who has no prejudices and excludes nothing; for everything, according to him, can, and ought to, profit us. This is not want of prudence on his part, for he is careful to tell us not to read the Heptateuch nor the books of Kings in the evening, lest weak imaginations should be troubled during the night (Rule, ch. 42); not that these books are suppressed, but simply read at other times.

Apart from these wise exceptions, he intends us to read each book straight through, without passing over anything: *integrum ex ordine legat* (Rule, ch. 48)

A counsel of the utmost importance in practice, but which, as we need hardly say, implies that we have at our disposal the time necessary for profiting by reading made under such conditions. Otherwise, if, for example, we have to read something quickly in preparation for half an hour's meditation, we run the risk of passing the whole time in vain research, without finding anything which may serve as a spiritual repast.

On the contrary, how naturally meditation follows from reading made under the conditions indicated by St Benedict! There, we have plenty of time and are not hurried. We read a page, or perhaps we read two, before we find anything which specially attracts us; but the time will certainly come when the soul is kindled and begins to be interested: some phrase, or even a single word, will suffice to fix the attention. Then, like men who have just discovered a vein of precious metal, we dig farther, searching the innermost depths of that phrase and extracting all its virtue.

This is meditation, natural and unprepared, springing simply from the contact of the soul with truth.

But this consideration will not stop short at a purely platonic state: love mingles with it, and will aspire to carry out in practice the consequences springing from the manifestation of truth. If the subject be one of those great verities which especially furnish food for admiration and joy, love will knock at the door of our Heavenly Father that it may obtain the full enjoyment of that which it has sought in reading and found in meditation. And how does love knock? By prayer, frequent, short, and pure: *Brevis debet esse et pura oratio* (Rule, ch. 20). Jesus cannot resist the soul which knocks thus; He opens to it, and visits it in these happy moments by the gift of contemplation. This word need not frighten us. Dom Guéranger defines it as "the state to which God, in a certain measure, calls every soul that seeks Him." These visits are momentary glimpses of the boundless horizon of eternity, intended to help us to pass from faith to vision.

Perhaps this mode of intercourse with God may seem hardly compatible with our busy lives. It is good, at least, that we should know what was the life led by our fathers, and that if the inspirations of grace call one or other amongst us to follow it, he may be able, from time to time, to catch a glimpse of the way. Some day we shall be old, and for most of us after labour will come comparative rest; and then we shall be glad to remember that we can spend a longer time in the things of God, in accordance with the spirit of the Rule, and our traditions.

And even now, have we not Sundays and feast days, in which more time is left us freely to attend to prayer and spiritual reading?

How good it is, then, to steep ourselves in that atmosphere of sweet and silent contemplation, whose charm our forefathers knew so well how to appreciate! How good it is to taste that wondering joy, which flows from the clear sight of truth—*gaudium de veritate*! (St Augustine, *Confessions*, 10., c. 23).

Happy those souls, who in the midst of a worn-out and materialistic world, keep unbroken the chain of those more intimate communications between Earth and Heaven! Happy the monk who shall deserve, by the fidelity of his actions and the lifting up of his heart in prayer, to be associated with those long generations of contemplative souls, who at the present day are scarcely found outside those cloisters where, withdrawn from the world, dwell the privileged spouses of Christ! This life is the precious jewel of the Church of God, her crown and her flower here below: one day it will be her fairest fruit in Heaven.

# IX
# MONASTIC POVERTY

*Omnes etiam qui credebant erant pariter,
et habebant omnia communia.*
"And all they that believed, were together,
and had all things common" (Acts 2:44).

WHENEVER WE SEEK in the religious life for that feature in which it most closely resembles that of the first Christians, we shall find it always in one thing, and that is the common life, having all things in common; and in that which is the result for each individual, the holy dependence of poverty. Other characteristics—the spirit of penance, obedience, assiduity in prayer—will be reproduced, even outside the religious life, to the end of time. But—except in some Socialistic Utopia—we cannot conceive of the absolute community of goods, save in a religious association. There alone is charity strong enough entirely to eradicate the concupiscence of the eyes, one of the three great evils which, St John tells us, is to be found in all that is of the world. Neither the friends nor the enemies of God make any mistake upon this point. The former, when they wish to bring back some religious institute to its first fervour, seem instinctively to feel that the basis of all lasting reform must be the return to the "common life". The name itself is recognized, for in certain countries a reformed monastery is called *a convent of common life*\*, in contradistinction to *a convent of private life*†. Then, again, do we not constantly see, when anti-Christian sects want to make an end of the

---

\* *Conventus vitae communis.*
† *Conventus vitae privatae.*

religious Orders, that they know beforehand that their wisest course is to make it impossible to possess goods in common?

The reason is that it is exactly this community of goods which gives solidity to any religious congregation, which assures to it its recognized place, its social position; and ecclesiastical authority never grants the canonical erection of a monastery, until its numbers have vindicated their means of subsistence. Some will say that this is a very paltry consideration. It may be so, but it is true to human nature itself. Even in the Church, as Ullathorne, Bishop of Birmingham, loved to repeat, the spiritual can hardly prosper (except in miraculous cases) without the good estate of the temporal. And again, was not the precise end of these miracles to provide supernaturally those indispensable resources for which natural means either did not suffice, or were voluntarily neglected for some special evangelical end?

Here we must make a distinction between poverty as it is understood in the mendicant Orders, and monastic poverty as it was seen in the Church before their time. The Franciscan, filled with a holy passion for the nakedness of Jesus crucified, throws himself, heart and soul, into his life of voluntary privation; for in absolute poverty he sees the principal element of his sanctification. He considers it, then, chiefly in its negative aspect, the absence of all prosperity, and rather from a personal point of view, as a means of himself attaining perfection. From that perfect profession of poverty which he intends to make himself, he would deduce but one consequence for his brothers in religion, for he would bind them like himself, to the strictest poverty, not only as individuals, but as a body. The convent can no more possess the smallest coin as its own than can any of the brothers. This is that touching privilege of holy poverty, always more valued by the Patriarch of Assisi and his spiritual posterity than all the other favours granted them by the Holy See.

This manner of looking at religious poverty was a new phenomenon, until then unknown to the law of the Church.

It was to make the mendicant state, occasionally practised before that time by some heroes of sanctity, the common law of a whole institution, much in the same way as Rancé, in the seventeenth century, subjected all his religious to a perpetual silence, until then observed only by certain individual types of primitive asceticism. Nevertheless, it is this Franciscan idea of poverty which has prevailed almost universally in the Church during recent centuries, so much so that we have come to profit by it ourselves. It is from this, for instance, that we get the *title of poverty*,* in virtue of which we are ordained; formerly we were considered as the regular clergy of our monastic churches, and, in consequence, ordained *for the title of the monastery*†.

But this is only a detail. The important thing is to understand that poverty is, above all, a social virtue, as well for monks as for the early Christians. It was certainly under this aspect that it made its appearance amongst the faithful. The text in the Acts is most emphatic upon this point, showing the suppression of individual property as the result of fraternal charity. Let us look again at the fourth chapter of the Acts: "And the multitude of believers had but one heart and one soul: neither did anyone say that aught of the things which he possessed was his own, but all things were common unto them. For neither was there anyone needy among them. For as many as were owners of lands or houses sold them, and brought the price of the things they sold, and laid it down before the feet of the Apostles. And distribution was made to everyone according as he had need." Here the primitive conception of poverty in Christian society is clearly expressed: its motive

* *Titulus paupertatis.*
† *Ad titulum monasterii.*

power is charity; its condition, the surrender of all personal rights of possession; its effect, the abolition of poverty by the equitable division of common property.

On the other hand, it is evident from many passages of the Rule that St Benedict had constantly before his eyes these verses of the Acts, and wished them to become the great law of his monasteries. Thus, without excluding the right of postulants to distribute everything to the poor before entering—a right, moreover, which was part of the Evangelical ideal, he nevertheless gives us to understand in many passages that to make a gift of their property to the monastery where they are received is perfectly legitimate. And this being the case, it is curious to observe that he, so liberal and so generous, so supernatural in his views, did not think that he could dispense, even in the interest of souls, with the ordinary precautions of human prudence. He speaks of solemn donations, of legacies made in due form, even specifying the eventual employment of the *usufruct*.* It is precisely this putting all things into the common stock which enables the Lawgiver to exact from the individual the most absolute renunciation of all property. This renunciation of everything, even of his body and his will, goes so far that, like the first Christians, he may not call anything whatsoever his own (Rule, ch. 33). But, in return, each one shall have the right to "expect from the Father of the monastery all that is necessary" (ibid.), the duty of this latter being to provide by his justice and foresight against any excuse arising from necessity. If the monastery itself is poor, if, for example, it cannot provide wine, still, poor as it is, everything must be in common, so as to render all murmuring impossible.

In this, Benedict is faithful to his practice of excluding noth-

* *usufruct*—the right to enjoy the use and advantages of another's property short of the destruction or waste of its substance.

ing and letting none of God's gifts be lost; and he has on his side the doctrine of the most illustrious Fathers of the Church, who are no less spiritual on this point than on the subject of mortification. They constantly teach, in fact, that riches, no less than poverty, may help to raise the soul to God. They point out that Abraham, in the midst of all his riches, was no less poor in spirit, and therefore no less pleasing to God, than Lazarus, begging the crumbs from the table of the wicked Dives; and when the day of reward came for the beggar, it was the bosom of the rich Abraham that received him. Our blessed Father, too, understood that all gifts come from God, even natural ones, and if rightly used may lead to Him, and therefore he set no limits to the increase of the material goods of his monasteries, and he has even promised this increase as a reward provided that we are faithful in seeking first the kingdom of God.

We know what a noble use our Order has made of these riches, whether by enhancing the dignity of Divine worship, or by giving efficient help to the many needs of the Church and of society. It has often been said that relaxation came into our Abbeys as the result of riches. This was the case sometimes; but as a general rule, history has proved that monastic communities have never been more fervent within, or more beneficent without, than when at the zenith of their power and riches.

Every period of relaxation, on the contrary, coincides with a lessening of material resources, with wastefulness, and alienation of all kinds; and every time that a great reformer has been raised up by God, however detached from worldly considerations he may himself have been, he has made it his first care to re-establish the monastery in all its ancient temporal rights. His zeal in this respect may have surprised us, but he knew better than we the spiritual advantages resulting from the good ordering of temporal affairs.

But we must always remember that the practice of voluntary poverty has ever been regarded in the Church, in accordance with the example and counsels of Christ, as a powerful means of personal sanctification; and, as we might expect, St Benedict never intended to deprive his monks of it; far from this, he encourages them to run joyfully the way of absolute renunciation. Not only may the monk, even without seeming to want for necessaries, be as poor in spirit as the most destitute of beggars; but, furthermore, if drawn by the grace of God, nothing need prevent him from actually refusing even necessary things, the moment he has his Superior's leave to do so. He may even beg from those outside, or in the community itself. In this regard there are degrees enough of humility to satisfy the ambition of the most generous souls. The least that the monk can do is to cut off all superfluity, and to this his Rule expressly obliges him—*Superfluum amputari debet* (Rule, ch. 55).

Thus we see that the holy Lawgiver always follows the same rule of conduct. In all things concerning the community as a whole there is to be nothing singular or too rigorous, nothing to frighten the weak; on the contrary, especially in this matter of poverty, there is rather a certain general air of comfort. But this comfort, on the part of each individual member, is the fruit of a truly fraternal charity and of the absolute renunciation of the least appearance of superfluous enjoyment. It leaves room for the free action of grace, which will surely suggest to elect souls a more complete despoiling of self, as complete as may be found beneath the rough serge of the Franciscan or the rags of the meanest beggar.

It is this spirit of individual privation which gives life to poverty as understood and prescribed by St Benedict. We may say boldly that correspondence to grace in this matter is one of the clearest signs of the progress of the soul of the religious towards union with God and with Christ crucified. It is, as it were, the result of all those truths deeply engraved in that soul by faith: the fragility and little worth of all transitory things, the absolute sufficiency of the Supreme Gift, which is God; the dishonour to which sin has reduced us by making us dependent on inanimate creatures; the happiness of dying to everything in this life, in imitation of Him Who died naked upon the Cross. Are not these reasons more than sufficient to keep us from drifting into that commonplace life of shelter from all want, with which the world, always malicious, yet, even in its malice, sometimes just, has long reproached those who have dedicated themselves to God?

The world has been punished by the very things for which it scoffed at us. It reproached us with our riches, and robbed our fathers; and now these same riches which have passed into hands incapable of making a good use of them have become a new source of trouble to society, by the absorption and exploiting of the poor by the rich, of the working man by the capitalist, of the needy by the careless and selfish possessor.

This is, in great part, the cause of that extreme agitation which appears to threaten us with a revolution, less sanguinary, perhaps, than that of the eighteenth century, but even more radical. On all sides the wealthy are striving to arrest this movement where it is dangerous, and to support and direct it where it is just.

It is the duty of the Benedictine Order to interest itself in these great conflicts in which the future of civilised nations is at stake. Its place is already marked out in the battle which is about to be fought on a new field; and that place, if only we show ourselves worthy of it, will be in the front rank. How and why is this? Because, even independently of any direct influence on our part, our life is, in itself, the most perfect realisation possible of what society desires and seeks today, without those disadvantages and excesses which society is powerless to avoid. What do those who in any degree recognise the need of social reform actually desire?

The more equitable division of the goods of fortune; the softening of the lot of the poorer classes; the prevention, as far as possible, of the "exploiting" of the poor by the rich, of the weak by the strong, of one who can hardly find his daily bread, by him whose life is steeped in luxury and effeminacy. That is what is desired by all those who have the good of their brethren at heart and are not entirely absorbed by selfishness.

Some go much farther, and imagine that they can bring about the community of goods. An idle dream, doubtless. Nevertheless, we monks have found the secret of its realisation. Here is matter of reflection for the world, which is compelled to ask itself why it can never realise what we find not only possible but perfectly simple. If it were not altogether blinded by its prejudices, it would recognise that all the difference between itself and us comes from the fact that we have not the same starting-point. With us the moving principle is charity, that perfection of brotherly love which makes such inequality of fortune intolerable. The spirit which mostly actuates the world is envy. Now, what is envy but covetousness, which is the exact opposite of charity? After this we need not wonder at the difference of result.

Granted that many of these Utopians are actuated by a sincere love of their brethren, yet the whole world could never bring together love sufficient to carry out in itself that which it acknowledges in us, but it can at least draw from our example this great and necessary lesson, that the result of all its efforts will be in proportion to the amount of Christian charity which it puts into them.

This is not the only lesson offered to the world by those monasteries where true poverty is observed. Beside covetousness, which urges the rich to guard and continually increase their riches, and the poor to seize upon them by every possible means, there are still two great obstacles to be overcome before anything like a balance can be restored in contemporary society: the unbridled luxury of one class, which values wealth only as a means of enjoyment; and the desire of another, to be rich without labour.

Now the monastic life plainly shows the absurdity of these contradictory tendencies. With us everyone is a possessor; and sometimes the amount of property thus held in common may seem large to the outside world; but no matter how closely we look at it, we shall never find the least trace of anything that can truly be called luxury. No doubt there will be found the traditional character of grandeur and stateliness which befits the fulness of Divine worship and the social presentment of the life of the Church, but the individual luxury which the world loves and pursues before all else, that luxury which feeds the threefold concupiscence which is destroying it, will be searched for in vain among us so long as we are true monks.

It is the same with work. People often imagine that having enough to live upon we pass the whole day, when we have finished our prayers, in a kind of sanctimonious idleness, having done absolutely nothing to earn our bread. Whatever good we may do, we shall never completely eradicate this prejudice. But it is all the more necessary, especially in these days, to prove to the world that work is really held in honour amongst us. Our lay brothers have not so much to fear on this point, neither they nor the Trappists being much maligned; for their work, being more material, is more readily appreciated by the outside world.

We choir monks must show all those who do not deliberately shut their eyes that our work is no less laborious and assiduous than that of our lay brothers; and to do this, we must devote ourselves zealously to every kind of activity for the general good of the Church and of society in which the will of our Superiors may call us to take part. It is true that we no longer have those royal endowments which enabled our fathers to distribute such bounteous largesse, but we can do much by our work. We need only think of those Solitaries of Egypt, who, though reduced to earn their poor daily fare by the work of their hands, yet found means to send out ships, laden with provisions, to distant regions suffering from famine.

And are there not many touching instances, both in the life and Rule of our holy Patriarch, of that burning charity which the monk should have for his brethren the poor? It will be enough to cite that fourteenth "instrument of good works": *To recreate the poor*\* (Rule, ch. 4). Most expressive word! For truly it is that, the "re-creating" of the poor, the truly poor; that mysterious creature which Christianity alone knows how to understand and honour. Instead of a poor man, conscious of his high dignity, happy in his modest and dependent condition which makes him like to the Son of God, we have got a poor man impatient of all inequality, full of hate and menace, preferring to the work which would ennoble him, an idle indigence which debases him, and which he will use presently as a grievance against society. Has not the lot of these poor creatures been full enough of tears and sufferings but hate must be added to it? Only love, stronger even than in the past, can cast out this spirit of hate. Let us "re-create" the poor, showing him by the way we treat him that he ever bears the Christ within him; let us say, *Deo gratias* (Rule, ch. 4.) whenever we hear his plaintive voice; knowing that, if needs be, we must, as St Benedict has shown us, deprive ourselves even of necessaries to give to him. Thus, with God's help, will be manifested to the world the justification of that form of poverty which we have embraced.

\* *Pauperes recreare.*

# X
# DISCRETION AND BREADTH OF VIEW

*Dividebant omnibus, prout cuique opus erat.*
"They divided (their possessions) to all,
according as everyone had need" (Acts 2:45).

THERE ARE TWO special passages in the Rule, in which St Benedict explains his conception of monastic poverty: these are chapter 33 (*Whether monks should have anything of their own**) and the second half of chapter 55, which treat of the distribution of necessaries. Now, it is remarkable that in both the blessed Father hastens to add, commenting upon it in his admirable way, the phrase which occurs in two places in the Acts of the Apostles: "Distribution was made to everyone according as he had need" (Acts 2:45; 4:35).

We can never lay too much stress upon the importance of these few words and the manifest influence which they exercised on the holy Lawgiver's whole life and precepts. This it is which distinguishes our monastic equality from the unjust and visionary equality which men lay claim to as one of the fundamental principles of social reform.

The equality of our democrats is absolute equality for all and each, whatever may be his duties, and consequently his rights; it is like the bed of Procrustes, which had to fit both tall and short, at the risk of mutilating the one and violently stretching the other. Monastic equality is proportional, taking account of physical and moral differences, and the gifts both

* *Si quid debeant monachi proprium habere.*

of nature and grace; meting out to each his work and rest, and the alleviations of body and soul, according to his strength and need—*Every man hath his proper gift from God, one after this manner and another after that.*\*

It must be confessed that our age, despite all the good in it, is, unhappily, a levelling age. Not only have men shorn the official representatives of authority, as well as the highest ranks of the upper classes, of whatever might enhance their prestige in the eyes of the populace, but they have set themselves (especially in countries visited by the Revolution) to ruin all institutions capable of exercising any kind of superiority. This is true of all great corporations, whether religious, scientific, or even simply of working men; and it is true also of individuals. Modern society, so proud of having proclaimed the rights of man and raised the dignity of the individual, has found no way of enlarging the base without at the same time lowering the apex. The benefits of instruction have been made as general as possible; but little care has been taken to secure to exceptionally gifted minds their full intellectual development. We are told (and with some truth) that the frequent anomalies of the Middle Ages would be impossible now; that manners are gentler, that philanthropy is everywhere extending its influence! But where shall we find today, save in the inexhaustible fruitfulness of the Church, those types of heroic virtue of which past ages offer us so many examples?

Again, we must honestly admit that the tendency to universal levelling is gaining ground day by day, even in ecclesiastical society. All rule is a burden; all influence, however lawful and kindly, is displeasing; anything unusual, however reasonable, becomes at once a subject for criticism and grumbling. If the formation and direction of the mental faculties is in question, people at once show a curious mistrust of everything which

\* *Unusquisque proprium habet donum ex Deo: alius sic, alius vero sic.*

may contribute to raise the intellectual level; they never cease talking of the dangers of science; they discourage, or at least they do nothing to encourage, the efforts of those who are trying to start any movement for lifting men's minds out of the mere commonplace.

It is the same with regard to spiritual perfection; any departure from the beaten track is intolerable, and men will do their utmost to avoid it. Generally speaking, however, they are content with this negative attitude; but when it comes to anything in the least degree out of the common (to say nothing of those generous enterprises to which the Holy Spirit still urges great souls), they put themselves on the defensive, and, if needs be, will stifle and extinguish it. So much is this the case that it may be said, with even greater truth than in the seventeenth century: "Nothing is admired but mediocrity.... Whoever succeeds in escaping this will infallibly find the teeth of the majority fastened in him" (Pascal, *Pensées*, 29. 21). This goes by the name of discretion and equality.

No, this is not equality. What it really is was once proclaimed by a great Bishop before the representatives of democracy, who were obliged, in spite of themselves, to applaud him: "True equality is not that which brings down all superiority and all greatness to one rude and barbarous level, but that which permits all that is noble and generous to germinate, to expand, and to rise" (Dupanloup, "*Discours pour la liberté de l'enseignement supérieur*," quoted in his *Life*, by Lagrange, vol. 3., p. 308). We need not seek far for the true idea of discretion, after what our holy Patriarch has said of it in his Rule—that Rule which St Gregory so justly calls "a masterpiece of discretion." This discretion in nowise consists in a rigid uniformity—an idea as false as it is dangerous. Discretion does not confine itself to preventing excess: that is an incomplete idea; we can sin against discretion by defect no less than by excess. Discretion, as revealed in the teaching of St Benedict, is that wonderful tact which is the first requisite for distinguishing the needs and the powers of each soul, its strength and its weakness, its resources and its deficiencies, what it actually gives and what it is able to give; and consequently the means to be employed to draw from that soul all the profit possible for God, its brethren, and itself.

From this we can see how many qualities are hidden under the simple name of discretion, and how wisely the Lawgiver calls it the mother of virtues—*Discretion is the mother of virtue*\* (Rule, ch. 64). It requires, first of all, a breadth of thought, feeling, and action, extremely rare in our days; it implies, in fact, that we should appraise each thing according to its value in the eyes of God, entering closely into the science and providence of God. He alone is Supreme Discretion; none can equal Him in the art of dealing with each soul according to its needs, leading it to its supernatural end, whilst still respecting its free-will. Man's ideal should be to approach as closely as possible to this Divine art, manifested in every detail of the relations of the world with God. But it is in the cloister, above all, that we must expect to find this ideal realized in the highest degree possible on Earth, for there souls are more delicate and more transparent; and, on the other hand, the natural and supernatural lights are more abundant, enabling us, as the Apostle says, to see all things under their true aspect—*The spiritual man judgeth all things*† (1 Cor. 2:15).

Now, the first result of this abundance of light should be to make us appreciate and admire the wonderful diversity in the works of God. Just as in the vast extent of the forest no two blades of grass are exactly alike, so we must not expect to

---

\* *Discretio mater virtutum.*
† *Spiritalis judicat omnia.*

find in the great human family two types absolutely identical. Does this prove that one is less perfect than the other? This may sometimes be the case, but generally it is difficult to decide, for these imperfections are often balanced by advantages which are wanting to other creatures seemingly more perfect. It is clear that wherever this difference of perfection is not a consequence of the disorder caused in man by sin, it comes from the direct will of God, for it is the source of that magnificent variety which we see throughout creation.

Grace, superadded to nature, has an equal share in this providential diversity. It is grafted upon nature, and doubtless perfects it, making it bear fruit which it would never have produced by itself, but leaving it its own temperament and its personal and distinctive characteristics. Thus we have saints made of quite different materials; setting aside faith, hope, and charity, the common possession of them all, and the habitus of the moral virtues, we might almost say that each one represented in himself alone an original creation. There have been saints of the highest intellect, and saints whose natural abilities were very limited; saints whose faces were always lit up with tenderness and joy, others with severe countenances, furrowed with tears; saints who have fled from martyrdom, others who awaited it calmly, or even ran to meet it; saints who so hated public dignities and offices that they fled or prayed for death in order to escape them, others full enough of fraternal charity to allow the burden of the episcopate, and other ecclesiastical dignities, to be laid upon them. The lessons of the breviary sometimes speak of saints who have watched with tearless eyes by the death-bed of those most dear to them; others (and those not the least illustrious), like Bernard and Augustine, have there shed tears, which their genius has made immortal.

It does not seem, therefore, as if God had ever meant His

grace to be a uniform mould for the destruction of all individuality. This destruction, the same eloquent Bishop whom I have already quoted, calls in some sort "a crime" (Letter to Montalembert, quoted in Lagrange's *Life of Dupanloup*, vol. 1, p. 413). And Dom Guéranger once said, in speaking of some saints more strict than others: "Ah, my daughter, the Holy Spirit acts upon what He finds." What is this but to say that the Holy Ghost does not deform nature, but conforms it to Christ; sometimes subdues, but never crushes; transfigures without disfiguring? We should seek in vain for a better model than the Holy Spirit to aid us in our dealings with souls. But the misfortune is that we all have within us our own little ideal, outside of which we can imagine nothing. It is said that artists involuntarily give their own features to those persons in their picture on whom they are bestowing most pains; and such is too often the case with those who have to deal with souls. Of course, the work will always bear the impress of the worker; but there is one way to avoid the ill-effect of casting all souls in one mould, and that is to widen ourselves.

Yes! Let us be *broad!* Most men have only fragments of ideas; let us endeavour to acquire the whole complete idea, for thus only can we help souls. Let us accustom ourselves to take a broad view of things; let us beware of making a counsel into a precept, a means into an end, a simple custom into an absolute rule. When we approach a soul, let us try to make sure that it has within it the love of God. If it has not, do not let us despise its natural qualities, but strive to complete them by grace. If the soul is in the friendship of God, resolved to hold it fast, and to make continual progress in it, other things, for which we might wish will not seem very important. The mind which judges things from this high standpoint is naturally indulgent, and is not easily surprised or disconcerted by imperfections.

Examples of the past, and its own experience, have prepared it for anything that may happen, so that it will not be too much scandalized even when faults are committed in the monastery. It was a man of God, a broad and strong soul if ever there was one, who said: "A bad monastery is not one where faults are committed, but one where faults go uncorrected."

I spoke just now of the power of the history of the past to enlarge the mind. Nothing is more true, especially for us monks; and this should give us a high esteem for the study of the records of our forefathers' doctrine and example. The mind can hardly travel on a better road. So long as we never come out of our own little corner, we do not understand the things that are passing in other countries, they do not exist for us. If we chance to see a man act in a different way from what would be done in our village, we are inclined to find fault with him, and laugh at him. It is the same with all minds which reading has not introduced into a wider circle than their own; they condemn and judge everything by their own standard. A knowledge of what has taken place in different times and countries would accustom them to judge more liberally of the persons and things of their own day. Thus the venerable Abbot Maurus Wolter found nothing of greater utility in the training of his young monks than the study and analysis of Mabillon's Annals, the writings of our own St Anselm, or some records from our venerable tradition of fourteen centuries. Seldom, perhaps, was the Founder of Beuron better advised than upon this point, for it has been well said that "an Order which does not live by its past has no future" (A. Danzas, *Études sur ... l'Ordre de s. Dominique*, préface). We must not, however, be too exclusive, even here. The past is past, and if it be good to question it for the secrets of wisdom and experience which it holds, yet, after all, our efforts must be for the present time and our own surroundings. Let us take a broad view in this as in everything else. There may be much to displease us, but also much that is praiseworthy, which we should frankly sympathize with and admire. Let us, in short, always look first for points of agreement, and not of difference—the only possible way to come to a fuller understanding of the truth. We must bring these principles to bear even on the *esprit de corps*, so legitimate in itself. It is well to love what we possess, and to think nothing better for ourselves; but that is no reason why we should rashly find fault with what is done elsewhere. It is almost incredible how some men, especially in the world, have narrowed the circle of what they love and esteem, until they have made themselves the one model and type of perfection.

One of the best ways of showing our discretion and large-mindedness, is to exercise a boundless and delicate compassion towards all; for all stand in need of it, and it is almost the only thing that we can give to our brothers at every moment of our life, whatever be our rank or office. There are many things with which only the Superior or one of his officers can provide me; if I have not sufficient clothing, I go to the brother in charge of the wardrobe; if I am hungry, to the cellarer; if sick, to the infirmarian. But if my physical, intellectual, or moral defects call for indulgence, if I need to be comforted and cheered, though only by an affectionate look, a kind, brotherly smile, or a friendly word, I ought to be able to call upon all my brothers, and to be ready at any moment to show the same charity to them. If the Abbot's authority has been entrusted to me in any degree; if, above all, the sacred ministry has invested me with what is most delicate and paternal in the exercise of that authority; then I must take to myself the counsels which St Benedict addresses to the Abbot, as he does to the cellarer, the guestmaster, the infirmarian, or the porter.

And how is this counsel summed up, but in this most necessary thing—mercy, indulgence, compassion? Yes, even among the manifold and minutely described duties of the Abbot himself, there is one which dominates all the rest, as oil rises to the top of any other liquid, and that is mercy: *But let him set mercy above justice*\* (Rule, ch. 64).

The Dominican Rule has been characterized as the "joyous Rule"; we might, perhaps, with even better right call our Benedictine code "the compassionate Rule." Can a single maxim, ever so little austere, be found in it, which St Benedict does not hasten to mitigate, so as to reassure any soul which has even the beginning of goodwill? When there is need for punishment or excommunication, what tender and compassionate precautions we find—the *sympaectae*†, those *secret comforters*‡; the example of the Good Shepherd, bringing back to the fold the lost sheep; all that system of spiritual medicine which must be tried, before having recourse to "the sword of separation".

And is not even the runaway monk to be thrice taken back on his simple promise of sincere repentance? Have we ever read elsewhere anything to compare with this for generous compassion? We might search all traditions, from the end of the sixth century to those times when ecclesiastical discipline appears most to take human weakness into account, without finding anything to surpass, or even to equal, the merciful large-mindedness shown by St Benedict. Only, perhaps, to some exceptionally great soul, an Augustine or a Gregory, has it been given to share this immense treasure of condescending charity. If it be true that the Benedictine Rule is a compendium—"a mysterious abridgement" of the whole Gospel—and

---

\* *Superexaltet autem misericordiam judicio.*
† *Sympaectae—Old and prudent brethren.*
‡ *Occulti consolatores.*

that the Gospel itself may be reduced to the one word "charity," it may be said that the Rule has found means (at least, in most cases) to epitomise still further; it is all compassion.

The exercise of this compassion is, in the main, only that "good zeal" which all monks ought to have and which will keep us from what St Benedict calls an "evil zeal of bitterness", from which so easily come self-complacent thoughts of duty accomplished, and our own exalted perfection. Nothing can be more contrary to the true spirit of the Gospel. The whole life of our Lord was a continual warfare against this "evil zeal," whether in the Scribes and Pharisees or His own disciples. The first schisms, those of the Novatians and Donatists, and the great modern schism, Jansenism, sprang from this zeal.

Doubtless we ought to hold fast to the fear of God, that indispensable foundation of the whole supernatural life; but still this praiseworthy sentiment must not make us forget the measure of compassion due to our neighbour. Fear is the first of the gifts of the Holy Ghost, but piety follows immediately after, to complete and moderate it. If we sometimes fear that this piety may be hurtful to the rigour of discipline, let us remember that reply of Odilo of Cluny, whom his contemporaries called *archangel of monks*\* (Mabillon, *Annal.*, I, 53, n. 113): "If I am lost, I would rather that it should be for having been too merciful, than for an excess of severity"—*Si damnandus sum, malo damnari de misericordia, quam de duritia* (*Cf. Vita*, auct Petro Damiani, Migne, 144, 930*a*). A touching maxim, echoed in Father Faber's words: "I am not saying it is easy to be a saint, but ... the saints are the easiest masters. It is because they are more like Jesus than other men" (*All for Jesus*, p. 182).

---

\* *Archangelus monachorum.*

# XI
# JOY

*Sumebant cibum cum exultatione.*
"They took their meat with gladness" (Acts 2:46).

AFTER HAVING DEPICTED that side of Christian life on which man is bound to God, participation in the Holy Sacrifice, liturgical and private prayer, St Luke indicates in general terms the rule which governed the relations of the brethren amongst themselves—that is to say, community of goods. He now comes to one of the details of daily life, the repast held every evening in some private house; and in two words he shows us its characteristic features—joy and simplicity. It is thus that he completes his picture, and that we will bring to a close this series of comparisons between the monastic life and that of the first Christians. Let us speak first of the part played by joy in a Benedictine Abbey.

What, then, is joy? Joy is not a virtue but the fruit of a virtue, and that the greatest of all—charity. It is the state of the soul in the presence of its beloved. It is love, but love in possession of its object, that *enjoying love*\* of which Saint Augustine so often speaks. It is a repose, a "passion," as the schoolmen call it, but a passion which shows itself by many signs both in soul and body; for example, that kind of trembling, that transport, that bounding of the heart, generally called in Scripture (as here in our text) *exultatio*; or, again, by those exclamations by which the soul expresses a joyous admiration which words are

\* *Amor fruens.*

powerless to render. It is the *jubilus*, the jubilation. All these signs together make up the state of gladness, *laetitia*, a word which expresses the many instinctive ways by which the joy of the heart, *gaudium*, is manifested outwardly. From this idea it follows that joy cannot be commanded; nothing is more unconstrained. A forced joy would be nothing but a grimace and an untruth.

This is why a smile is necessarily so short; if prolonged it ceases to be pleasing, because untrue. In the same way theologians teach us that contemplation, properly so-called, cannot last long; it is too nearly akin to joy; it is the *joy from truth*\*. Again, earthly joy is too free, too capricious in its action for us to expect it to last. The Psalmist compares it to an impetuous river flowing through the city of God. *The stream of the river maketh the city of God joyful*† (Ps. 45:5). If we desire to have this water of joy always welling up in our midst, clear and abundant, we must protect and enlarge its source, which is love. We may say of joy what we have already said of enthusiasm for the Liturgy, which is one of its first manifestations, that it is the barometer by which we may test the degree of charity in each soul, as in each community.

As we are bound to employ ourselves with a zeal unhappily too rare in these days, with the Divine praise, we have need, even more than others, to possess in ourselves an ample provision of joy. But even independently of this particular aspect of our vocation, we may say that the cultivation of this joy is an absolute necessity for all common life, because the perpetual contact with the same souls, each one laden with the burden (more or less heavy, but always real) of regular observance, may very easily become painful and wearisome to nature. Thence,

---

\* *Gaudium de veritate.*
† *Fluminis impetus laetificat civitatem Dei.*

unless we are very careful, will arise continual friction and annoyance, and incessant reasons for sadness. Add to these the imperfections peculiar to each individual, the differences of character, education and nationality—all that accumulation of troubles, corporal and spiritual, which each one must drag after him until his last breath; and it will be clear enough that such an assemblage of persons brought together in the religious life (monotonous enough in itself), and bound to stability of place, will quickly become intolerable even to the most courageous souls, if the Divine ray of joy do not come to aid them to bear the present by pointing to the future. At all times this joy has been the inheritance of good monks and fervent communities. St Antony, the founder of the cenobitic life, possessed it to such a degree that strangers could recognize him by it, amongst all the solitaries. We read the same thing of other illustrious monks, even the most austere. St Romuald, whose history contains details which terrify our weakness, had so joyous a countenance, that only to look at him made men glad. And even now the surest sign by which to judge of the fervour of any community is the joy reflected on the faces of its members, the gladness which gives life and spirit to every movement.

But, it may be asked, how shall we set ourselves to attain joy, since, being the fruit of charity, it cannot be directly acquired, like the virtues which are developed in us by exercise? True, but at least it is in our power to remove anything which may obstruct the sweet radiance of that Heaven-born spirit. It is charity which gives it life and nourishment; but this life may be continually increased by the reciprocal action of joy, on the foundation of charity which we already possess. I will explain. It is unquestionable that the first foundation of all joy, is our baptism. If we clearly understand the greatness of the gifts made to us in that ever-blessed hour—the communication of the fulness of eternal life in Christ; the Father making us His adopted sons; the Son, His brothers and co-heirs; the Holy Ghost, His living temples; the implanting in our inmost being of sanctifying grace, with its efflorescence of theological and moral virtues, of gifts and fruits—shall we not find here a never-failing source of joy? Each truth of faith is, in itself, a world of joy where the soul may ever find delight. Unhappily, most Christians are little used to consider the faith under this joyful aspect; indeed, from this point of view modern tendencies differ notably from those of earlier centuries. Let us glance at the various forms of our primitive liturgies. Certainly we shall find many expressions of humility and compunction—but the humility is joyous, and the compunction almost always ends on a note of triumph. Look at that great Friday itself, when it would seem as if sorrow should absorb all other feelings—is not that solemn adoration of the Cross the most enthusiastic of triumphs? Is it not at this very moment that the choir proclaims God the Holy, God the Strong, God the Mighty, and the joy which came to the world through the Wood of the Cross—*for behold by the wood of the Cross joy has come into the whole world?*\*

There still exists an ancient Office in which the Churches of Germany formerly celebrated the holy Lance and Nails, which they gloried in possessing. This Office was fixed for Paschaltide, a time of joy and triumph; and each portion reveals the holy enthusiasm which inspired both melody and words. It was the same with the Offices consecrated to the other Instruments of the Passion. Let us turn from these to the optional Offices for the Tuesdays of Septuagesima and the Fridays of Lent; we find them full of exclamations of sorrow, of *Heu*, of *Proh dolor*, *Proh nefas*, an unceasing call to sighs and tears. And it cannot be denied that most of these compositions are in harmony

---

\* *Ecce enim propter lignum venit gaudium in universo mundo.*

with the general tendency of the pious souls of our generation. There is the same change in iconography. We have all seen the ancient type of Crucifix, where Christ is as if enthroned in all the royal apparel of His majesty. He is clothed; the crown upon His head is no longer the crown of thorns, but the heraldic crown of honour; gold and precious stones have replaced the blood and wounds of Golgotha. In a word, Christian faith has exercised its ingenuity, in restoring to Jesus all of which He was despoiled for love of us, in this supreme moment of His victory; and so has made the Cross the richest and most triumphal ornament of our churches. And if the crosses are still veiled during Passiontide, it was primarily because the brilliance and richness of these crosses—as well as of the reliquaries and the images of the saints—would contrast too vividly with the austere majesty of these last weeks of Lent. Nowadays we are too realistic to care for this kind of crucifix; our dull senses must have all the gaping wounds, the thorn prints, the ribs laid bare, the flesh torn, the blood streaming from every part. It would be difficult to understand the Providential reason of this transformation, but that Dom Guéranger brings it out so well in his notes on Saint Paul of the Cross. It is none the less true, however, that that atmosphere of joy in which society was reared, during the thousand years that the Church was free to model it after her own likeness, has become very much rarefied in these later days. It is certain that we can no longer stand the amount of joy which never wearied our forefathers. Look at those holy days of obligation, formerly so numerous, which are always having to be reduced: that great Octave of Easter which once filled whole cities with mirth, but of which one or two days are now quite sufficient for all the rejoicing we want.

What was Eastertime itself but a continual feast, the prolongation of Easter-day, a long period of joy, intended to equal, if not to surpass those forty days of Lent, consecrated to penance and fasting? Whence comes it, that even the Easter festival itself is so little understood by the majority of Christians? Christmas at least is observed by everyone, thanks to its Holy Eve, and Corpus Christi, too, because of its procession; but why is it that Easter—the culminating point of the whole Christian year—is hardly now (save officially) "the solemnity of solemnities," but that we have forgotten to seek in the crowning mystery of Christ and His Church the treasures of spiritual joy which it contains?

No doubt one great cause of the diminution of joy in our day is the neglect of mortification; other causes are the lessening of hope, the more selfish trend of modern currents of thought, the forgetfulness of the eminent dignity of the Christian, and of his intimate participation in each of Christ's mysteries. All that Christ did to lessen the distance between our souls and God, and to bring us into friendship with Him, is lost to sight, and seemingly forgotten; man seems almost as much a stranger to God as before the Incarnation. Far otherwise thought the Christians of the first ages, with their greater realisation of their Divine sonship, their brotherhood with Christ, their dignity at once priestly and royal. Each great solemnity, as it came round, was the occasion for extraordinary outbursts of rejoicing, for a sort of *tripudium*, to use the consecrated term, in which the spiritual joy that filled the hearts of the faithful was manifested in a fashion perhaps somewhat exuberant.

Many events have in their turn contributed to crush this joy, once common to the whole Christian world. First, the religious revolution of the sixteenth century, which, strange to say, has never taken firm hold except among the colder nations of the north of Europe. Under pretext of bringing everything back to the austere simplicity, from which the Church of Rome was supposed to have departed, all regions were wrapped in a gloomy silence, which is felt to the present day. Then came Jansenism, which by its blasphemies against the Sacred Blood of our Lord prepared the way for the philosophical Deism of the eighteenth century. Christian good sense has triumphed, and a beneficent reaction has set in; the Sacraments are received frequently, and moral theology seems to have widened to its utmost limits; but, all the same, how difficult it still is to make people see our religion as it is in reality, the pre-eminent source of joy! As a general rule, they confuse it with different practices recommended by one person or another—practices which may suit those who have invented them, but will not necessarily suit everyone else. They want all Christians to be of one pattern, overwhelming them with particular examens, interminable devotions, sometimes with absolute fads, instead of saying to them simply: There is Christ; you will find everything in Him—study Him, go straight to Him; He is the Truth and the Life, He alone can give you happiness; He is the Way in which you must walk. The chief reason why men no longer know how to "rejoice in God" is because we no longer know how to turn them to Christ.

And yet this joy is, in itself, such a powerful element of sanctification! It has been said: "Two things are necessary for holiness, pain and pleasure" (Pascal, *Pensées*, 28. 35). Let us listen again to the eloquent Bishop of Orleans, explaining to a soul under his direction how joy, as well as grief, may draw us nearer to God. "There is one Scriptural word which I want to say to you, a secret which I wish you to learn. 'I have run in the way of Thy commandments,' it is said in the beautiful 118th Psalm, 'because Thou hast rejoiced my heart.' Grief draws us nearer to God, but so does happiness; we are carried along with a breath, all we have to do is to hoist our sails. We have to make efforts when we are suffering; when we are happy we need hardly do more than let ourselves go. Open, dilate your soul—it is God, it is God. ... All these joys of the present moment, my child, are like the morning dew which God sheds upon us, before the burden and the heat of the day. The flower drinks in the dew with rapture: it is its way of thanking God" (letter of Mgr. Dupanloup, quoted in his *Life* by Lagrange, vol. iii., p. 403).

The great monastic founders of our time have used no other language to their monks. Dom Maurus Wolter, the pious founder of Beuron, considered that it was the chief duty of the Abbot to spread joy around him; and certainly, only to look at him, to meet his glance, to see the smile upon his lips, was sufficient to fill the beholder with joy. The founder of the French congregation, in his turn, said to the nuns of Sainte-Cécile: "When I hear you laugh I am filled with pleasure, and the good angels rejoice!" And, on another occasion, "My little daughters must be an Alleluia from head to foot." The source of this joy was, according to him, the enlightened use of the Sacraments, familiarity with the Scriptures, love of the Psalms, and knowledge of the never-ending gifts of God to His Church. And as all this is more or less related to the Liturgy, he made that the basis of his monastic reform, desiring that each great solemnity of the year, each Sunday even, should bring to his monks an increase of this spiritual joy. His teaching upon Sunday, in his conferences at Sainte-Cécile, deserves particular mention here. "Sunday," said he, "belongs to God in a special way; therefore we must offer it to Him in a different manner from other days. On this day your life should resemble that of the blessed—you have more time for prayer, the soul has freer scope, and can better seek God. It is very important not to lose the Sunday. It is for you to put these general maxims into practice, and to make Sunday an entirely holy day." And he added most emphatically: "I wish to impress this upon you, so that you may observe it."

But we have said enough upon that joy which flows directly from the love of God. In our family life there is another element of joy, no less powerful, and in certain cases even more efficacious. I speak of that charity which we ought not only to bear to ourselves, but to show to one another. The joy which comes from the love of God is a joy of hope, for the beloved Object is still hidden from our eyes. On the contrary, we can, and we ought, to take pleasure in the company of our brothers even now, as we shall do one day in Paradise. Now when the object is present, the joy is, for that very reason, more complete. Would that we could clearly see what causes we have for joy in each one of those chosen souls whose destiny God has deigned to link so closely with our own! It would seem sometimes as if God purposely threw a veil over the merits of each, so as to blend the qualities of all in one harmonious whole. How often has it happened, for example, that we have learned some touching trait of one of our brothers whom we should never have given credit for such lofty virtue, only on his deathbed, or when we were absent from the monastery. Then we say: How is it that I never saw the beauty of that soul? How many occasions I have lost of rejoicing at God's gifts to one of my brothers!

This is true in general of those who, in the readiness of their hearts, are serving God side by side with us. Nevertheless there are certain souls to whom Jesus has given the grace to exercise in a more visible manner this contagious influence of joy. These are they who are not afraid of showing, so far as modesty and obedience permit, the charity which burns within them—who have a "face of love." How shall we describe this face of love? Monsignor Gay, one of the most remarkable ascetical writers of our time, defines it thus: "Its brow is serene, its look ingenuous, calm, benevolent, sweet, compassionate, full of attraction; its lips parted, ready to smile, its ear easily inclined; its voice sympathetic; it exhales simplicity and peace like sweet perfume; itself at ease, it makes others so. This loving soul goes on its way always giving—or rather, it always gives itself."

This last quality, to give oneself, is, before all, the distinctive feature of those apostles of joy in the monastery. Is there one amongst us who does not feel a thrill of gladness at the sight of a brother constantly absorbed in the perfect practice of that counsel of St Paul—*Let every one of you please his neighbour unto good*\* (Rom. 15:2)—always seeking what he knows is most agreeable to his neighbour, whatever can help and console him, whatever may give him joy? It is especially from the youngest monks that one has a right to expect that sweet perfume of flowering vines, of which the sacred Canticle speaks: *the vines in flower yield their sweet smell*† (Cant. 2:13). Then the soul, however cast down it may be, breathing this aroma, renews its strength and generosity, and says with the spouse: "Let us run in the odour of Thine ointments" (Cant. 1:3).

"Our Lord," said the Abbot of Solesmes, "has a great tenderness for souls thus striving to shed happiness around them, and they advance with giant steps." This is the true Benedictine spirit: *Let none follow what seems good for himself, but rather what is good for another*‡ (Rule, ch. 72). Let us recall the admonition to the cellarer: if he cannot give what is asked, let him at least give a good word, a word of peace, consolation, and joy (Rule, ch. 31). All who are charged with the distribution of anything whatever should give especial heed to this point: they must show by their countenance that it is a joy to them to give, to distribute anything to the family of God, aiding as much as possible, and even forestalling the needs of their brethren.

\* *Unusquisque vestrum proximo suo placeat in bonum.*
† *Vineae florentes dederunt odorem suum.*
‡ *Nemo quod sibi utile judicat sequatur, sed quod magis alii.*

Finally, we must all give ourselves to one another, we must show our happiness at being together, our pleasure in the society and conversation of the others at permitted times. We must never let it be thought that the hours of common recreation are burdensome. If we find the rare intervals in which we are together in this life a weariness, can we really desire to be all together in the next? There it will be always festival, always joy, always recreation; there, "Alleluia!" will be ever upon our lips as in our hearts—*Alleluia will be all our joy*\* (St Augustine, Sermon 252, n. 9). Here on Earth we say it as travellers, to comfort our weariness; but hereafter we shall sing it as an added charm to the repose of eternity. Here it is faltered by hungering love—in Heaven it will be chanted by satisfied love in perfect modulation. Let us then go forward singing, and let us sing as we go. Let us march, let us go forward—*Sing and march*† (St Augustine, Sermon 256, n. 3). Let us sing with joy, and by joy let us go forward in love.

---

\* *Totum gaudium erit Alleluia.*
† *Canta et ambula.*

# XII
# SIMPLICITY

*Cum exultatione et simplicitate cordis.*
"With gladness and simplicity of heart" (Acts 2:46).

WE HAVE SEEN how St Luke has associated simplicity of heart with the joy which, as it were, seasoned the daily actions of the first Christians. Indeed, these two dispositions always go together; the Holy Scriptures also love to mention them one after the other. Thus David: *Joy to the right of heart*\* (Ps. 96:11); and Solomon: *I also in the simplicity of my heart, have joyfully offered all these things*† (1 Paral. 29:17); and in many passages of the Acts we find these two things brought together in the same way. We may remember our Lord's injunction to His Apostles: "Behold I send you as sheep in the midst of wolves. Be ye therefore wise as serpents, and simple as doves" (St Matthew 10:16)—*Et simplices sicut columbae.* Hardly has the Shepherd left His sheep when the wolves fall upon them. The High Priests, alarmed at the rapid spread of the Gospel, summoned the Apostles to appear before them. "How is this?" they said. "Have we not expressly forbidden you to teach in that name? And behold, you have already filled Jerusalem with your doctrine!" What was their reply? What did St Peter do, he who with one word had just struck Ananias and Saphira dead? They remembered the precept of Jesus, and used no other weapon than simplicity. "Judge ye," they answered, "if

---
\* *Rectis corde laetitia.*
† *In simplicitate cordis mei laetus obtuli universa.*

it be right to obey man rather than God." Their simplicity was punished by scourging. But what was the end of it all? Joy—*They went rejoicing.*\*

Having spoken of joy, let us now say something of its natural companion—simplicity. Simplicity is the exact opposite of complexity. Complexity is not evil in itself; it implies an imperfection which could not exist in God; but in truth, all creatures, even the most perfect, are complex; and if there be one creature more complex than all the rest, it is man, uniting as he does in himself all degrees of created being—from his intellectual nature, which makes him like the angels, down to the gross material existence which he shares with the minerals. Only, if a being composed of such diverse elements is to remain beautiful, these elements must be brought back to unity, and that is what makes of human complexity such a marvellous whole; for all its parts, all its powers, emanate from one and the same force, which contains them all, commands them all, sets all in motion, and that is, the reasonable soul, the essential form of the body.

We may illustrate this by the phenomenon of the sight; that also is a kind of complexity, for we have two eyes; but the qualities of each eye being transmitted by the nerves to a common centre, the duplicity of the organ in no way interferes with the simplicity of the act of sight. It is the same with the simplicity of the moral sense. It was this very organ of sight which our Lord chose as a simile, when He wished to impress upon His Apostles the importance of simplicity. "The light of thy body," He told them, "is the eye. If the eye be healthy" (literally, if it be single—that is, in its natural state, as it should be to fulfil its office properly), "thy whole body will be lightsome," and all the other members, under its direction, will perform their functions without disorder. This cannot be if the eye be

\* *Ibant gaudentes.*

diseased, if from any cause it cannot see straight or correctly. According to our Lord's teaching, then, this simplicity dwells above all in the intention. It is not always easy to define exactly where it is, or where it is not, for there is nothing so secret as the intention, nothing so entirely within the domain of God. To see into the depths of the heart, is a prerogative which our Lord Jesus Christ often brings forward as a manifest proof of His Divinity.

It is the peculiar characteristic of simplicity that we often think we have found it, where there is in reality only deceit and consummate art; and oftener still, an excessive timidity—which, after all, is not a fault—a sort of awkwardness, native or acquired, or perhaps some slight dash of originality, has been enough to prevent our recognizing simplicity where it really exists, although hidden by those defects of manner which will hardly be got rid of until the last hour of life.

Simplicity is in the intention. But what is the intention? It is a seeking, a movement towards something, a direction given to the powers of the soul—*tendere in*. In the Christian life it is to seek God—in other words, to seek truth and justice; it is to refer everything to this end, to be simple in oneself, neither wishing to be, or seem, or do anything, except in the truth. This is the meaning of that striking expression so often used by St John: *Do the truth*\*. It is in fact the same thing that the author of Ecclesiastes calls the whole duty of man: *seek God*.† Taking that idea as our starting-point, we can see already that we ought to aim at simplicity with a special zeal, since it is the first condition, in reality the only one which St Benedict requires for the reception of his novices—*If he truly seeks God*.‡

---

\* *Facere veritatem.*
† *Deum quaere.*
‡ *Si vere Deum quaerit.*

Simplicity, then, is not foolishness, as the false world would have us believe; on the contrary, it implies a clear perception of the sovereign end of human life, and an energy which can aim straight at that end, without wearying, or turning aside, or going back. All this is the exact opposite of foolishness. How is it, then, that the world understands nothing of true simplicity? Because it does not know the end; or, if it does perceive it, it has come from its habit of deliberately turning away from it to lose and despise even the idea of its duty in relation to this supreme end.

From unity the world has turned aside to multiplicity. Its distracted mind roams from one belief to another, treating adherence to any one of them as antiquated or intolerant; it gives its heart to the highest bidder, and is surprised that others can keep a straight course without being caught, like itself, by the allurements of pleasure, riches, or honours, or any other form the passion of the moment may assume.

The simplicity of a Christian is based upon his faith, by which he adheres unhesitatingly to whatever the Supreme Truth has revealed to man. In our times nothing is more necessary for monks than that they should possess this faith, full, broad, solid as a rock. We may make certain concessions to the world on other points, but in the matter of faith our duty is to sacrifice nothing. And this faith we must extend to every detail of life, to our relations with our brethren, and, above all, with our Superiors. This again, is one of the characteristic features of our Rule. It is this spirit of faith which makes us see Christ in the Abbot, in the sacred vessels of the Altar, in the most humble utensils of the house of God. It is faith which makes us value the opinion of the youngest of our brothers, for it is to little ones that God often reveals His best; faith, which encompasses us with the Divine Presence, as with a shield;

which reminds us, in hours of prayer, that we are before the throne of His adorable Majesty, encircled by His angels; which moves us to serve our brothers, to care for the sick, to entertain guests, as though we saw Christ Himself. If a stranger sees anything to find fault with, the spirit of faith will suggest to the Abbot that he may have been sent for this very thing. In short, nothing will be done or said within the monastery which does not proceed from faith, and help to increase it.

We should accustom ourselves to look with this single eye of faith at the smallest details of our practices and ceremonies—for example, the shape of our habit and our tonsure, our profound inclinations, or any other point of our monastic or liturgical customs. That sometimes certain speculative doubts, certain personal preferences for different practices should arise in the mind, is perfectly natural, and so long as we do not insist upon them against the will of our superiors, there is no great harm done. But it is fatal to stop at such trifles, for it very often means drawing back. Let us accept *en bloc* and with the simplicity of faith all the small consequences of the one great act of our profession. Here, each one of us can speak from his own experience. Which are the good vocations—those that triumph over every obstacle? If a subject comes to the monastery to seek God only, without disturbing himself about aught else, we say at once: "He will do well, nothing will stop him, or at least nothing will make him look back; he will go straight to God." But when an aspirant to the religious life besieges us with questions: "What time do we get up? What is the ordinary diet? How much time is there for conversation? When does one begin to study? How soon can one become a priest?" we see at once, from the importance which he attaches to all these petty details, that he is one who cannot give himself up simply. Now this is, as we have seen, the principal, indeed the whole, duty of a monk.

We are thus forcibly reminded of the first movement which follows conversion of heart: *What shall we do, men and brethren?** For obedience, the total abandonment of self to God through the Abbot, is precisely what stamps the monk's life with the seal of true simplicity. Through this all his being is fast bound to God: his intelligence, his heart, every movement of his senses. Then it can be said of the monk that he is perfectly simple.

We must be simple, too, with our brothers, and here especially we need clear sight to discern in them through all the defects and imperfections of nature that supernatural grace for which we should love them in the strict theological sense of the word.

The first thing to be avoided is suspicion. Mgr. Gay somewhere says that if God could feel rancour, it would be against suspicious souls. We may certainly say that it is impossible for such souls to be simple in their forced relations with their neighbours. Their neighbours are to them a kind of shifting sand on which they can make no progress. They would like to be able to believe in some quality which they think God has put into their brother's soul, but they immediately suspect a snare.

"Perhaps," one will say, "this brother may be weak, subject to this or that fault, and if I show him that mark of affection or esteem, it may be a temptation to him. Or perhaps he dislikes me, perhaps he wishes to advance himself at my expense, and is jealous of my success!" What misery all this is! And there are few miseries more difficult to cure! In most cases the best thing a suspicious man could do would be to shut himself up in some hermitage where he would no longer have his neighbour as the food and victim of his suspicions.

We may say, generally, that the best way to be simple and just towards our brothers is to look more at what they desire to be than at what they are; not dwelling upon those little faults

\* *Quid faciemus, viri fratres?*

which they themselves are the first to lament and to atone for and blot out by repentance. Of course, there are cases in which it is necessary to take notice of the real imperfections of a subject; the Superior, for instance, must do so before entrusting anyone with an important office.

Such cases apart, let us think only of that in him which is eternal, of that which we hope to find again in him in Heaven. This is the true aspect, which does not change with every incident of the journey of life.

Again, we must be simple with our neighbour in the way we show our feelings towards him; our marks of respect and affection must come straight from the heart. Of course, we must show those outward signs of deference which are prescribed by our Rule or our customs; but do not let us go so far as to be stiff and ceremonious about everything. There is nothing so chilling as to bring this official character into the simplest relations of daily life; it takes half the youth and freshness out of it.

Especially let us avoid the exaggerated use of titles of honour, one of the surest signs of a period of decadence. Suppose, for instance, that a religious, venerable for his age or his dignity, were to call a young monk only just ordained, "Your Paternity"; in what a false position this inversion of characters would place him! Let us follow here what the Rule prescribes, "Let the younger brethren reverence their elders, and the elder love the younger" (Rule, ch. 63). In his chapter on "The Instruments of Good Works," St Benedict says: *To reverence the old, to love the young*\* (Rule, ch. 4). Here is enough to do away with the cold stiffness of which we have just spoken, and to make each one's part easy to him.

Flattery is another enemy to simplicity. True, it can hardly exist in a monastery, or even among Christians, except in such

\* *Seniores venerari, juniores diligere.*

outward forms as extravagant or unseasonable praise. But even that is too much, and will displease all straightforward and simple natures. With regard to Superiors, every act of adulation would, in the first place, make it more difficult for them to fulfil that indispensable precept which the Rule imposes on the Abbot in particular: *Let him always distrust his own frailty*\* (Rule, ch. 64); and secondly, it would cause fatal discontent in the rest of the community. With reference to this, we may recall those words of Melchior Canus, one of our most learned theologians, concerning the highest dignity with which any man can be invested on earth: *Peter has no need of our lies; he has no need of our adulation.*† St Paul also, that noble and true soul, calls God to witness that he has never used flattery, even in speech: *For neither have we used, at any time, the speech of flattery, as you know... God is witness*‡ (1 Thes. 2:5).

And, to make an end of what concerns simplicity towards our neighbour, let us ever have as our motto two words which well become the servants of Christ—frankness and courtesy.

Frankness is one of the noblest words in our language. It is the transparency of the soul, the shining of the heart through the face; it is the good conscience in which there is no dissimulation, no disguise, no affectation. Perhaps there is no quality more highly appreciated, even by the worldly, or which more surely finds its way to the heart. Let a sensible man, who is also a man of feeling, find himself in the company of a number of persons, all strangers to him, and he will be attracted instinctively and by some irresistible movement, towards the one with the frankest expression and most unconstrained manner.

---

\*   *Suamque fragilitatem semper suspectus sit.*
†   *Non eget Petrus mendacio nostro, nostra adulatione non eget.*
‡   *Neque enim aliquando fuimus in sermone adulationis, sicut scitis... Deus testis est.*

Such is the credit which frankness enjoys, especially in our time, and it is, perhaps, one of the best sides of present-day society, that it makes so much of this beautiful quality. It stands to reason that this frankness must be neither rude nor brutal; it must have its natural companion, courtesy, that unaffected Christian politeness which is never out of place, even in a monastery. It is written of Hugh of Cluny that he made his monastery truly a *cloister of angels*\* (*Vita St Hugon.*, auct. Hildeberto, Migne 159, 885*a*). The code of politeness observed by the elect in Heaven should be the rule for every Benedictine community. There is always something to be done in this regard, and our progress will be in proportion to our advancement in grace; for there is nothing in which the work of grace in completing nature is more visible. There is no soul, however small its progress in grace, which is not also a delicate soul, full of all the refinements of considerate and sincere politeness.

We must not only be simple with our neighbour in everything, but simple with ourselves. Do you ask how? By thinking and acting towards ourselves according to what we know ourselves to be in the light of God; with both the good points and the defects of our nature; with our sins, but also with the graces which we have received from Heaven; with all our weaknesses, but also with the gifts which the Divine mercy metes out to each one of us. To know ourselves thus in our totality, is not, says St Augustine, the sign of a soul puffed up with pride, but of one that would not be ungrateful: *Non est haec superbia inflati, sed confessio non ingrati* (St Augustine in Psalm 85, n. 4). Once let faith in the indispensable action of grace be firmly rooted in the soul, and there is nothing which need surprise it, either in the gifts which it may receive from Heaven or the duties to which it may be called on Earth. It will

\* *Deambulatorium angelorum.*

put self altogether aside, and think only how to "magnify its Lord who is working within it"—*operantem in se Dominum magnificant* (Rule, prologue).

This is that true humility and humble simplicity of which St Benedict speaks in his sixth degree. "Let us accustom ourselves," says Dom Guéranger, "to receive the greatest gifts from the hand of God, with simplicity." Should we be called by our Superior, or the choice of our brethren, to some employment which might alarm our humility, let us at once quiet our perplexed conscience by the recollection that the truly simple monk should be ready to occupy even the Abbot's place, if called by God, with no more ceremony than the novice would use about " the office of humility, " when once the novice-master had made choice of him for it.

But if we make distinctions, if we accept this and excuse ourselves from that, as too high for us, we are counting upon our own strength, instead of, as justice requires, referring everything to God and to His grace.

But in our own imperfections we shall find still further occasion for the exercise of simplicity. Considering our weakness, we need be surprised at nothing; if we are, it is a sign that we hardly know ourselves. Neither need the like infirmities astonish us in others. We must, of course, aim generously at the perfection congruous to our state; but let us remember also that this perfection consists, before all else, in love, and so be on our guard against that deplorable tendency of many devout persons to regulate the exterior before the interior, too often at the latter's expense. Do not let us try to edify our neighbours by a studied manner and rigid postures whose conventional character betrays itself at once. It is noteworthy that St Benedict has made that perfection of manner which comes from perfect interior humility the highest step of his ladder; a proof of his wisdom and power of observation, for if he had required conformity to this ideal from beginners, it would have been at once intolerable and false.

To make an end—nothing is more foreign to the Benedictine character than falseness and duplicity. The world, even in our own day, recognizes in our Order this special grace of frankness and simplicity; and in the practice of Christian prudence so especially necessary for these times, there must be nothing to the prejudice of that hereditary virtue of uprightness and sincerity, beloved alike of God and man.

It has been said by an English writer that to be simple and loving is to be born a king.

The influence which the monk exercises in the world of souls comes in great measure from this lovable simplicity. In Heaven also, after the resurrection, it will be one of the attributes of the Blessed; if, according to the beautiful definition of St Augustine, it is true that "simplicity consists in having nothing that we can lose"—*dicitur simplex, cui non sit aliquid habere, quod vel possit amittere*. Strictly speaking, no doubt such simplicity belongs only to God; but what is the primary object of our monastic life, what was that of Christian life in its beginnings, but to seek to draw ever nearer to God, if we may but touch Him at last—*seek God, if happily they may feel after Him*\* (Acts 17:27)?

---

\*   *Quaerere Deum, si forte attrectent eum.*

www.ingramcontent.com/pod-product-compliance
Lightning Source LLC
Chambersburg PA
CBHW020324010526
44107CB00054B/1973